Rock & Wall Climbing

Rock & Wall Climbing

Garth Hattingh

First published in 2000 by
New Holland Publishers Ltd
London • Cape Town • Sydney • Auckland

All enquiries should be addressed to:
Stackpole Books
5067 Ritter Road, Mechanicsburg, PA 17055.

2 4 6 8 10 9 7 5 3 1
First edition

ISBN 0-8117-2916-8

Library of Congress Cataloging-in-Publication
information is on file

Publisher: Mariëlle Renssen
Commissioning editor: Claudia dos Santos
Editors: Laura Milton, Gill Gordon
Designer: Mark Jubber
Illustrator: Danie Jansen van Vuuren

Consultants: Greg Pritchard (Australia)
Neil Champion (UK)

Reproduction by Hirt & Carter (Cape) Pty Ltd
Printed and bound in Singapore by Craft Print (Pte) Ltd

Although the author and publishers have made every effort
to ensure that the information contained in this book was
correct at the time of going to press, they accept no
responsibility for any loss, injury or inconvenience sustained
by any person using this book.

Cautionary note
Although wearing a climbing helmet
is a matter of personal choice, the
author and publishers recommend
that a suitable helmet is worn on
any occasion when the climber may
be exposed to the risk of a head
injury occuring.

Author's acknowledgements

I would like to thank all my friends and colleagues for many good times in the hills. To the team at New Holland Struik — Laura, Mark, Gill and the rest — many thanks for your tactful help. Special thanks also to Willem and Keith, for bearing with me in times of stress.

Publisher's acknowledgements

The publisher would like to thank Geoff Ward of Outward Ventures, Simon Larsen of Ram Mountaineering, and the Mountain Club of South Africa, for providing information and advice; as well as Clinton and the other climbers who participated in the photo shoots.

Contents

The Climbing Game

telling your friends that you're going rock climbing is often met by peals of laughter, disbelief or ridicule of some sort. A frequently-held view is that rock and wall climbing is for death-wish lunatics only, a bizarre macho sport in which you traverse vast distances of treacherous terrain, only then to climb hundreds of metres of featureless, overhanging rock — in a blizzard. Climbing can, of course, come to this, but for the majority of climbers it is simply an exciting and pleasant way of temporarily escaping the monotony of everyday life — a thrilling physical experience during which you have some fun whilst engaging in the absorbing business of calculated risk.

A calculated risk

One of the greatest climbers in the world, Reinhold Messner, describes climbing as 'controlling risk' — if the risk factor is too great, then you are 'out of control', and danger replaces adventure. In climbing, the aim of the exercise is to become expert enough to assess situations accurately, and retreat — or not even begin — if the risk of a serious accident is too high. Coming from Messner, who has summitted all of the 8000m peaks, most without oxygen, and pioneered some of the world's most extreme climbs (and lived to tell the tale) this is very good advice.

The aim of this book is to help teach you how to reduce the risk factor, without losing the exhilaration and adventure inherent in, and essential to, climbing. It focuses on rock climbing, only touching briefly on other forms of climbing such as artificial walls, snow, ice and 'aid' climbing. The basic principles, however, remain the same for all forms of climbing. Merely reading this book, and following the advice to the letter, will, of course, not guarantee your safety — gaining experience, using your common sense and seeking advice and help from expert climbers will both enhance your enjoyment of climbing and reduce the chances of an accident.

above and right DESPITE THE POPULAR IMAGE, CLIMBING IS NOT REALLY ABOUT RISK AND DANGER, ALTHOUGH THE PRESENCE OF DANGER DOES ACT AS A STIMULANT OR INCENTIVE TO SOME. TO MOST CLIMBERS HOWEVER, CLIMBING IS MORE ABOUT PERSONAL FREEDOM AND MEETING PERSONAL CHALLENGES. CLIMBERS ALSO REFER TO THE 'SLOW ADRENALINE BURN' THEY EXPERIENCE WHILE UNDERTAKING A CLIMB.

It's all in the game

In reality, climbing is just a game. No one *has* to climb mountains or rocks — it is done as a pastime providing great enjoyment and simply, as the saying goes, 'because the rocks are there'. Certainly some people have made climbing their livelihood, in the same way as professional golfers or football players, for example, make their living from sport — but the vast majority of climbers participate in the sport purely as a game.

A keen climber, Lito Tejada-Flores, in his landmark essay, *Games Climbers Play*, outlined, in a tongue-in-cheek fashion, the various types of climbing and the rules that apply. Rules are generally made to 'control' a game, but also exist to prevent the game being 'too easy' — for instance, being able to run with the ball in your hands would make a mockery of soccer, whereas it is part of the game in rugby football. In the same way, climbers have largely unwritten, but nonetheless well-known rules to 'level the playing field' — or, rather, to 'steepen the mountain'. If you are climbing a huge alpine face, with bad weather looming, then to pull up on or stand on pieces of equipment placed in rock cracks might be deemed acceptable, whereas to do the same on your local short crag would probably bring disapproving looks from other climbers. This is not to say that you cannot choose your own way of doing a climb — but some things would simply not be considered 'good style'!

Let's examine some of the games climbers play:

Bouldering

This is possibly the simplest game of all, requiring the least equipment and, for this very reason, it is subject to some of the most stringent unwritten rules. Essentially, all that is needed is a low boulder and a climber. Boulders can vary from half a metre (1.6ft) to a terrifying (and possibly unwise) 10m (33ft) in height. If you want to add 'equipment', you may opt for using special rock shoes — sticky-soled, tight-fitting, sensitive footwear (see page 18) that allows you to take advantage of every ripple in the rock — and chalk, a powder used to dry off the fingers and palms (see page 21) and thus increase their power of adhesion.

Now the rules begin. In truly serious bouldering, the use of a rope is 'out', you cannot stand on pieces of gear inserted into the rock, your partner cannot support you physically, and you must keep to the acknowledged route (on many boulders, for instance, there are numerous different boulder problems sharing a very limited space).

For many climbers bouldering becomes an all-consuming passion, and some can happily spend hours in the cellar at home, where a small home-built overhanging panelled wall is used to take the place of a natural boulder. Of course this is fine, but the joy and beauty of being outdoors is lost.

Some offshoots of bouldering are the following:

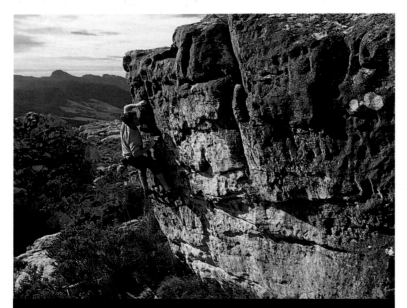

above BOULDERING IS FUN, IT IS A CHEAP WAY TO BEGIN CLIMBING, AND IT IS SOCIABLE. IT IS ALSO VERY DEMANDING ON FINGER TENDONS, NEEDS GREAT STRENGTH AND POWER, AND IS HIGHLY GYMNASTIC. PROVIDING YOU TAKE CARE NOT TO TRY TO COPY THE GURUS TOO FAST, AND STICK TO THE EASIER PROBLEMS INITIALLY, IT IS A SUPER WAY TO START OFF YOUR CLIMBING CAREER.

Free solo (unroped) climbing

In essence, free solo climbing is bouldering taken to new heights — quite literally. Solo (unroped) climbing involves climbing to any height with none of the usual climbing safeguards. This unfettered form of climbing can hold great appeal, as it allows the climber to move fast and fluidly.

This is certainly not recommended as a way of beginning your climbing career, as many a climber, including renowned experts, have met their death on free solo climbs. If all goes smoothly, and the climb is well within the physical and mental capabilities of the climber, then free solo climbing is exhilarating, a pure form of the art. If the slightest thing goes wrong, however, your attempt may end in tragedy.

EXTREME FREE SOLO CLIMBING IS BEST LEFT TO THE EXPERTS — HIGH ON A ROCK, WITH NO PROTECTION, THIS IS NO PLACE TO SUFFER FROM UNCERTAINTY OR FEAR!

Deep-water soloing

Perhaps a slightly more 'sane' way to engage in free soloing is to climb above water. Many parts of the world, including the Calanques in France and parts of the British coast, boast long stretches of cliff bordering deep sections of ocean. These can have traverses which stay at a reasonable height above the water for miles on end. Not only do you experience testing and sustained traversing, but also the benefits of a fall that may involve a wetting and perhaps a long swim — but not severe injury or death. It comes as no surprise that this kind of climb is particularly popular on warm summery days! Remember, however, that water can seem as hard as steel if you hit it from 10m (33ft) or higher, and that the hazards of cold water and large waves are just as substantial as sharp rocks below — or, in some areas, unfriendly neighbourhood sharks! Educate yourself well about your chosen climbing environment by consulting guidebooks, and speaking to people with local experience.

DEEP-WATER SOLOING CAN BE AN EXTREMELY ENJOYABLE WAY TO CLIMB, WITH THE CONSEQUENCES OF A FALL BEING NO MORE SERIOUS THAN A WETTING IN COLD WATER AND A LONG SWIM BACK.

Buildering

Here the name says it all — this kind of climbing is done on man-made structures not built for climbing purposes, but that lend themselves to great sport nonetheless. Beware, though, as climbs like these can — and do — lead to fines or arrests. Architects and property managers take their responsibilities very seriously, and convincing the court that you 'were only doing a little wall climbing on the bank' might not be all that easy. Climb these structures, by all means, but do seek approval first. (And sometimes it may even be a good idea to check timetables — there is a well-known case of a climber who had to cling precariously to a steep railway embankment as a slow goods train rumbled along below him for what seemed like ages.)

Climbing walls and rock gyms

Rock gyms and artificial walls are extremely good places to start your climbing career — they usually have equipment to rent and trained staff on duty to offer advice and to make sure that you don't go wrong during the tricky starting phases. Most gyms provide a wide range of routes of varying difficulty, and offer you the opportunity to learn from other climbers. Many countries where sport climbing is popular offer good facilities, with a particular abundance in Belgium, France, the UK and the USA. The main danger of rock gyms is that enthusiastic beginners often push their limits

A GROUP OF CLIMBERS HAVING SOME FUN (AND A GOOD FINGER WORKOUT) BUILDERING AWAY ON THE NATURAL STONE WALLS OF A MOUNTAIN HUT.

A WELL-EQUIPPED ROCK GYM THAT HAS IT ALL — SUPERB BOULDERING, GOOD LEAD WALLS AND PLENTY OF ROUTES TO PLEASE EVERYONE FROM RAW BEGINNERS TO THE HARDIEST CLIMBER. ONE OF THE ADVANTAGES OF ROCK GYMS IS THAT THEY CAN BE USED IN ALL WEATHER CONDITIONS.

too hard and too fast, resulting in muscle or tendon injuries (see pages 82–83). Poor belaying practices can also result in a number of avoidable accidents.

Most purpose-built centres for climbing started as small, basic constructions that allowed climbers to train all year round. Many of them, however, have developed into huge creations valued in their own right, and are no longer regarded as mere substitutes for the 'real thing'. Some climbers enjoy climbing gyms so much that they never leave the 'plastic' (as these walls are known) to head for real rock faces.

In certain cases, the 'wall game' can also have a set code of highly restrictive rules, where you may not touch this or that hold, for instance, or must stay to one side of a line. However, in a gym you are far freer to ignore these than on the rock faces — after all, you are there for training and fun!

Climbing competitions

The advent of climbing competitions has enhanced the popularity of rock walls and gyms, and the frequent media coverage has given a huge boost to climbing in general. In these competitions, the ascent of a set route with a carefully determined grade of difficulty (see page 92) has to be completed within a certain time limit. Climbers score points according to how far they manage to climb the route within the given limit — time is not a factor in determining your score, unless you run out of it!

Speed climbing events are a separate category, where a much easier route has to be completed in the fastest possible time. Many countries now have regular climbing circuits, which are particularly well-supported by school and college students.

Apart from local and national competitions, there are international events, including the World Cup circuit, and 'Invitation' events for the crème de la crème, held at places like Serre Chevalier in France, Snowbird Lodge in the USA and Arco in Italy. There are also annual World Cup events in the youth (under-13) and junior (under-19) categories.

Major competitions offer some good incentives, fame, fortune, and substantial prizes. In addition, competitions provide opportunities for safe climbing under controlled conditions, and offer pleasant social interaction. They do, however, demand rigorous training, immense self-discipline and motivation, and a cool head under pressure.

COMPETITION CLIMBING HAS INCREASED THE POPULARITY OF THE SPORT IN GENERAL, AS IT ATTRACTS SPECTATORS WHO WOULD NORMALLY NEVER SEE CLIMBERS IN ACTION. COMPETITION RULES GOVERN ROUTES, DEGREES OF DIFFICULTY AND THE TIME ALLOWED IN EACH CATEGORY.

Sport climbing

Sport climbing is a fairly modern climbing game — with its roots in France in the late 1970s. The Alpine areas of France had many climbs where guides had banged pitons (metal stakes) into rock fissures to offer protec-

THE FORM OF CLIMBING WHERE THE CLIMBER CLIPS THE ROPE INTO PRE-PLACED, FIXED ANCHOR POINTS IS KNOWN AS SPORT CLIMBING. IT HAS PROVIDED RELATIVELY SAFE, ACCESSIBLE CLIMBING TO THOUSANDS OF CLIMBERS, AND IS AN EXCELLENT WAY TO START OFF WHEN TOP-ROPING OR LEADING YOUR OWN CLIMBS.

tion to the leader in the case of a fall, and left these in place for convenience when guiding parties of climbers. Young climbers spotted the potential of this practice, and also started to protect harder, steeper routes — first with fixed pitons, and then with expansion bolts inserted into holes drilled in the rock. The advent of battery-powered drills and quick-set epoxy resins has led to more and more areas being bolted.

Most sport climbs are a single 'pitch' long (see page 56). This means that you climb up to a point from which your belayer (your partner, who belays or holds you, with the aid of a mechanical device — see pp 40-43) lowers you back to the ground. There are, however, many multi-pitch sport climbs, which allow you to climb for hours up a single route.

There are many climbs and certain types of rock which are best protected by bolts (see page 60), these being the only possible and reliable form of protection — and a good number of local authorities have agreed to specified areas becoming bolting areas, leaving other rock faces for the natural gear-aficionados (see next page). There is little doubt that the ease of the use of bolts has been responsible for a large increase in the numbers of climbers on rock faces, and there is ever-growing pressure to bolt more and more areas. The degree of real damage bolts do to the environment is debatable, particularly if one considers the impact of walking paths, trails, fences and even signs proclaiming 'no bolting'! In certain areas the banning of bolts is justified, though, and this must be respected.

Sport climbing has led to standards in extreme rock climbing improving dramatically, as here you can 'push your limits' until you fall, with little danger of the protection points giving way (although this can happen). Sport climbing often takes place on very steep overhanging rock, where tremendous strength, power and gymnastic ability are required to succeed. These skills, and the fitness resulting from numerous repeats of strenuous routes, transfer to long alpine routes or other natural-gear rock climbs (see next page), and there can be little doubt that many of these modern extreme climbs owe their existence to the techniques and power derived from sport climbing.

Natural-gear rock climbing

This kind of climbing is what most people still conceive of as 'real' climbing. One person, the leader, starts up a rock face, trailing one or two ropes. He or she places protection (referred to as gear) into cracks in the rock at intervals, and clips the rope(s) into these via snaplinks (carabiners). The second climber safeguards the first by holding the rope, usually via some form of belay device (see page 40—41). Once the leader reaches a suitable spot, he or she places more protection, attaches him- or herself, and then belays the second climber up to his or her level. The second climber removes all of the protection as they climb up, for later use.

This game too has rules, the most common being 'thou shalt not pull on, or stand on, the gear' (unless conditions are *really* extreme — only then may it be acceptable). It is customary, with these climbs, that

THE TRADITIONAL WAY TO CLIMB (ALSO CALLED 'TRAD' CLIMBING AND ADVENTURE CLIMBING), ALLOWS CLIMBERS TO MOVE OVER PREVIOUSLY UNCLIMBED PIECES OF ROCK, WITH NO PRE-PLACED GEAR SUCH AS BOLTS, AND IS THE WAY IN WHICH NEW, BIG CLIMBS IN FAR-OFF RANGES (OR EVEN SMALL LOCAL CRAGS) ARE TACKLED.

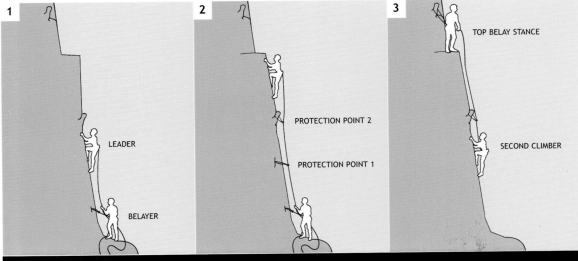

1   LEADER

BELAYER

2   PROTECTION POINT 2

PROTECTION POINT 1

3   TOP BELAY STANCE

SECOND CLIMBER

1 LEADER, ON BELAY, CLIMBS TO THE TOP OF ROUTE OR PITCH, PLACING PROTECTION (RUNNING BELAYS) AS HE OR SHE CLIMBS.

2 THE LEADER COMPLETES THE ROUTE OR PITCH AND TIES ON AT THE TOP BELAY STANCE.

3 THE BELAYER (SECOND CLIMBER) THEN CLIMBS, BELAYED BY THE LEADER, REMOVING THE GEAR AS HE/SHE GOES.

subsequent climbers will undoubtedly try to repeat the route in better style by free-climbing the moves that were originally done with the aid of the gear. For a really 'pure' ascent, you would not pre-examine the route on rappel or by seconding it, you would not have 'beta' knowledge — information gathered from other climbers specifying exactly how to do tricky sections — you would simply get there, and do the climb.

The great advantage of traditional (or trad) climbing is that one can climb any piece of rock, anywhere, with a relatively small amount of protection gear, providing the rock has a fair supply of cracks, fissures or 'eyes' into or around which to place the protection. The disadvantages are that some rock is too blank or friable (crumbly) to accept natural protection, and that the

gear you place yourself is usually more likely to pop (come out of the rock) under the force of a fall than if it was being held by fixed bolts.

Placing natural gear is both an art and a science, and it takes time to develop the necessary skills (see page 62). You would be well advised to spend a good deal of time practising gear placement before putting it to any real test! The gear is expensive, and you will need a wide variety if you want to protect all possible situations adequately. It is also far more nerve-wracking placing your own gear than simply clipping into pre-placed, solid bolts, so start off at a much lower grade than you would normally climb if you were using bolts.

Trad climbing techniques are used from small crags, via big wall and aid routes, to alpine-scale climbs.

CLIMBING ON AID PAST A DIFFICULT SECTION. A LARGE VARIETY OF PROTECTION GEAR IS OFTEN NEEDED FOR TRADITIONAL AND AID ROUTES.

GOOD EXAMPLES OF TRADITIONAL CLIMBING ARE FOUND IN PARTS OF THE UK, THE EUROPEAN DOLOMITES, AUSTRIAN TYROL, MANY ROUTES IN YOSEMITE AND OTHER PARTS OF THE USA, AND COUNTRY ROUTES IN AREAS SUCH AS THE CEDERBERG OF SOUTH AFRICA, THE GRAMPIANS OF AUSTRALIA AND THE DARRENS OF NEW ZEALAND.

Crag climbing

This is practised on small outcrops, some 20–100m (65-330ft) in height, with only a few pitches. A pitch is the length of one section of a climb, dictated either by the length of the rope normally used, or any natural features which lead to good belay ledges or which force a belay (such as a spot just before a large overhang). Crag climbing differs from sport climbing, not only in the lack of bolts, but in the tendency of crag climbers to walk or scramble down via easier pathways after a climb, rather than be lowered off by the belayer. Crag climbing is still the most popular form of climbing in a number of countries, including the UK, USA, South Africa, Austria, Germany and Australia.

Crag climbers are usually very particular about the rule of not using gear to provide aid, as this helps to stack the odds against the climber in a situation that usually has little other objective danger.

Big-wall climbing

In this sub-game, the object is to get a number of climbers (a pair, or a larger team) up a huge rock face by any reasonable climbing means. Often aid may have to be used to overcome blank or overhanging sections; that is, the climber pulls up, or stands, on slings attached to pieces of protection gear. Frequently this aid includes the odd bolt drilled into the rock.

A second important feature of this game is that other members of the team do not have to climb the pitch — they often ascend ropes fixed by the leader by means of mechanical ascenders such as

jumars (see page 72). In this way, they save both time and energy. On big walls, large amounts of food, water and survival equipment are normally hoisted up stage by stage in haul sacks.

The boundaries between the various games and sub-games are becoming increasingly blurred as climbers push the limits. Many older routes, where aid was previously used, are now free-climbed or even free-soloed.

OVERNIGHT BIVOUACS ON THE WALL ARE PAR FOR THE COURSE. BIG WALL CLIMBS ARE FAR MORE SERIOUS IN TERMS OF POSSIBLE WEATHER COMPLICATIONS, AND THE DIFFICULTIES OF RETREAT IN THE EVENT OF INJURY OR ACCIDENT OR THE PARTY'S INABILITY TO FINISH THE ROUTE.

Choosing Equipment

it is not necessary to possess a vast array of climbing gear and gadgets in order to enjoy climbing. However, when you think of all the wonderful experiences made possible by using equipment, it becomes clear why most climbers choose to use at least some form of gear.

To beginners, experienced climbers may seem to move swiftly and effortlessly across or up a rock face, making it seem so easy! Once they themselves are on the rock, though, it suddenly seems slippery and the grips are minute. How did the other climbers do it? Not only are they well practised, but they are probably using tight-fitting, high-friction climbing shoes and special powder to dry their finger tips and increase grip.

Climbing shoes

The correct rock shoe or boot will greatly enhance your climbing ability. The better the shoe, its fit, and the more suited to your type of climbing, the greater the improvement will be.

ELASTICIZED SIDES AND POINTED TOES ARE PAINFUL BUT POPULAR, AS THEY ALLOW THE SHOE TO BE TIGHT-FITTING YET STILL SENSITIVE.

The right all-purpose shoe

■ Fits snugly and tightly. Most shoes stretch after a while, so enduring a bit of pain at first is perhaps unavoidable. Climbers often choose shoes at least one or two sizes smaller than their normal shoes. It is usual not to wear socks, or only to wear thin ankle socks. Thick socks reduce sensitivity, and allow the shoe to move on your foot — which is no good if you're trying to balance on a tiny edge of protruding rock.

■ Has a semi-rigid sole which gives firm support to your feet and prevents them from being crushed in cracks. Check the support of the shoe yourself by flexing it across the sole — it should have as much give as an average good running shoe. Squeeze the toe — if it flops around, it will not help you during the learning phase of climbing.

■ Has a fairly large rubber 'rand' or strip of edging right around the sole (see below left) — about 2-3cm (1in) is ideal. This is a great help when feet are jammed into cracks and when an edging technique is used, and it helps protect the shoe or boot. Remember that as a beginner, you will wear out shoes or boots faster than experienced climbers, who have learned to place their feet precisely.

■ Could offer a bit of ankle support — the sides extending up to protect the ankle. (This is not as important as the other criteria mentioned above, however, and high-top climbing shoes are not common. If the climbing shoes you find have all the necessary qualities, but lack ankle support — then take them.)

right CHALK IS AMONG THE MANY ITEMS OF GEAR (SUCH AS ROPES, HARNESSES, SHOES, CARABINERS, SLINGS AND SO ON) THAT CLIMBERS USE TO HELP GET UP (OR DOWN) THE CLIFF IN SAFETY. FOR THE MOST PART THIS HELP IS INDIRECT — CLIMBERS DON'T HANG OR PULL ON THE GEAR AS A RULE, ALTHOUGH THERE ARE TIMES WHEN ONE DOES THAT (SUCH AS IN AID CLIMBING, RAPPELLING OR LOWERING OFF A CLIMB).

Specialized shoes

The areas in which you choose to climb (or are able to climb) may mean that you encounter mostly one particular type of rock or terrain. You may therefore, either initially, or at a later stage, prefer to buy a specialized climbing shoe. Some highly sophisticated footwear is available — including some amazing banana-shaped shoes that are surprisingly comfortable, and ergonomically designed to force your foot into a position where it gives maximum toe strength for use in pockets and on small edges. These shoes are not recommended for beginners, however, as they demand a good deal of strength from the toes and the soles of the feet — strength provided by small muscle groups that are only developed with much practice.

Extremely tight-fitting boots are not a good idea for use during long climbs (consisting of either multiple pitches or lasting for several days). On short, hard, technical routes, the advantage of increased performance can compensate for the pain and discomfort, and you can take the shoes off from time to time!

Taking care of your shoes

The sole should be kept as clean as possible, and should be cleaned after each outing — dishwashing liquid, water and a scrubbing brush are adequate. Despite regular cleaning, however, soles do tend to lose 'grip' with time as the tiny pores fill up with dust and grit. To preserve your shoes for as long as possible, the best practice is to keep the soles clean by not standing on dirt, and to wipe them with a brush or soft cloth before climbing a serious pitch. Many climbers take a small cloth or towel to stand on at the base of climbs, especially when bouldering. Empty rope bags (see page 30) are also useful for standing on in order to keep soles clean.

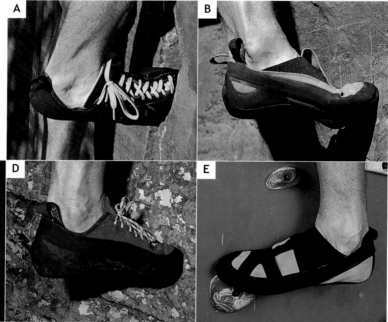

A FOR CRACKS: LOOK FOR A RIGID SOLE, GOOD ANKLE PROTECTION, AND A LARGE RAND ALL ROUND TO PROTECT AGAINST CRUSHED TOES.

B FOR FRICTION CLIMBING (E.G. SLABS): A SOFTER, MORE FLEXIBLE, TIGHT-FITTING SHOE ALLOWS FOR GREATER CONTACT. ROCK 'SLIPPERS' ARE OFTEN GOOD IN THIS KIND OF ENVIRONMENT.

C FOR FACE CLIMBING: ALSO CHOOSE A LESS RIGID BOOT, BUT WITH MORE SOLE FIRMNESS THAN SLIPPERS, TO ALLOW FOR THE USE OF SMALL EDGES OR POCKETS.

D FOR POCKET CLIMBING: YOU MAY CLIMB ON LIMESTONE OR SIMILAR ROCK, SO YOU WILL NEED A SHARP TOE PROFILE, WITH A HIGH HEEL RAND TO ALLOW FOR HEEL HOOKS.

E FOR CLIMBING WALLS: THE ON-OFF NATURE OF WALL TRAINING IN A ROCK GYM FAVOURS THE USE OF CLIMBING SLIPPERS, WHICH CAN BE SLIPPED ON AND OFF THE FEET IN A JIFFY. TAKE GREAT CARE OF YOUR SHOES, HOWEVER, AND ALWAYS REMEMBER THAT THESE SLIPPERS HAVE THIN SOLES WHICH WEAR OUT RAPIDLY, AND CANNOT EASILY BE RE-SOLED.

Types of chalk

In the world of climbing, the term 'chalk' usually refers to light magnesium carbonate ($MgCo_3.5H_2O$) with additives such as silica to provide extra grip.

A LITTLE CHALK ALLOWS FOR A POSITIVE GRIP ON SURFACES THAT MIGHT OTHERWISE BE TOO SLIPPERY.

And no — chalk is not there as a route marker, or for 'dot-to-dot' climbing, but to dry those sweaty palms and fingertips.

Climbers' chalk is available in blocks (which you have to break up into pieces or into a powder), in powder form, or as chalk balls (where the powder is encased in a porous sheath of stocking-like nylon or fine muslin). Chalk balls are becoming increasingly popular in indoor climbing gyms, where too much chalk dust can create a minor health hazard. Try out different types of chalk until you find what works best, and is most suitable, for you.

Types of chalk bags

Chalk bags come in a variety of designs — a large bag is useful for bouldering, whereas a small, compact one is handy for hard sport climbs where the less weight you carry, the better.

A good chalk bag

- Is large enough to take your hand easily when you dip it in.
- Has a tight drawstring closure to avoid chalk spills.
- Is fairly robust.
- Has a stiffened rim to prevent it from closing when in use.
- Has a fibre-pile or similar lining to ease the application of chalk to the fingers.

A cautionary word

Use chalk with discretion — many climbers overdo it, and use it as a psychological aid, not only for its intended purpose of drying the hands. It can become unsightly on rock faces, and is banned in some areas of the world (like the sandstone of Saxony, and at Fontainebleu in France). Respect these bans — often access to an area depends on climbers being aware of and following regulations, even if they seem silly or irksome (see pages 90-91). In both Saxony and at Fontainebleu there are valid, practical reasons for not using chalk — the porous sandstone easily becomes slippery when clogged with chalk, to the detriment of the climber.

CHALK IS AN EXTREMELY USEFUL AID, BUT USE IT SPARINGLY.

The harness

The next vital piece of equipment is the climbing harness and, once again, there are several options. Generally, the sit-harness — with a waist belt, leg loops, and some sort of front attachment system (see A below) is preferred to the full-body harness (see B below).

It is worthwhile spending a bit of money on getting a comfortable, well-fitting harness. Don't compromise — after all, you may end up 'hanging around' in it for a while! If you are still growing physically, or if you intend climbing in varying weather conditions, necessitating different kinds of clothing (for instance, shorts in summer and warm leggings in winter), then choose a harness with adjustable leg loops, as fixed-size harnesses are not adjustable.

Spend time finding a good harness. Ensure that the harness you choose can tighten firmly but comfortably above your hips and on your waist, so that you cannot slip out — even if you turn upside down (see safety tip on the next page). Insist on trying out several different harnesses in the store — and hang for a minute or two, to see how each harness feels. The job of the harness is to hold you firmly and securely, and to distribute any forces resulting from falls, rappels or lower-offs, to as large an area of your body as possible, and to the right places.

The best harnesses

■ Have a well-padded waist belt and leg loops, to increase comfort and to hold you securely.

■ Have leg loops that are independent of the main harness, but which pass through a belay loop on the front of the harness.

■ Have solid buckles, to securely accommodate the waistbelt when it is doubled back (see next page).

■ Have an adjustable system at the rear to lift or support the leg loops.

■ Have a good arrangement of fairly strong gear loops from which to suspend various items of hardware.

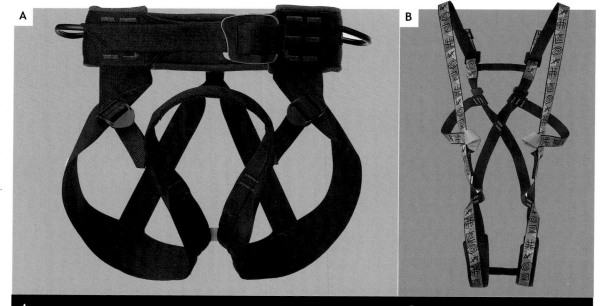

A FULLY ADJUSTABLE HARNESSES (ABOVE) ARE USED BY ALPINISTS AND OTHER EXTREME CLIMBERS, WHO MAY HAVE TO ADJUST THE SIZING FOR VARIOUS LAYERS OF CLOTHING, OR IN CLIMBING CENTRES WHERE MANY DIFFERENT PEOPLE MAY USE THE SAME HARNESS.

THE FIXED SIZE HARNESS (SEE PAGES 37 AND 55) IS POPULAR WITH MOST ROCK AND WALL CLIMBERS, AS IT IS OFTEN LIGHTER THAN ADJUSTABLE HARNESSES, AND OFFERS A BETTER, MORE COMFORTABE FIT.

B FULL-BODY HARNESSES ARE SELDOM USED, EXCEPT FOR ALPINE-TYPE CLIMBS WHICH MIGHT INVOLVE GLACIER TRAVEL AND CREVASSE RESCUE, FOR INDUSTRIAL USE, AND ON SMALL CHILDREN, WHO, LACKING A 'WAIST', CAN SLIP OUT OF CONVENTIONAL HARNESSES.

⚠ Harness position

If the harness you use has adjustable leg loops as well as a waist loop, *first* fasten the waistbelt tightly **above the hips** *before* tightening the leg loops — otherwise the result will be a dangerous, low-slung gunfighter-type fit, shown below. *Avoid* this at all costs.

⚠ Doubling back of the waistbelt

A number of first-class, experienced climbers — as well as many beginners — have come to grief as a result of not doubling back the waistbelt of the harness through the buckle. Often this happens when the climber becomes distracted half-way through the process. *Make sure you complete the full double-back process every time you fit your harness* (see **1** and **2** below).

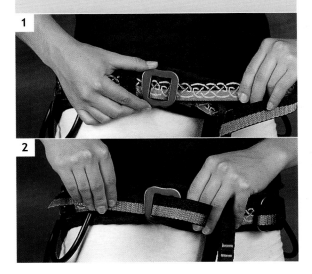

UIAA and CE Stamps

Virtually all climbing gear — harnesses, carabiners, ropes, slings, belay and rappel devices, helmets and other protection devices — should carry UIAA or CE approval, or both (see page 25). Look for these markings!

The UIAA (International Union of Alpine Associations) sets standards for climbing equipment that guarantee a minimum degree of safety. A UIAA stamp is a sign that the piece of equipment has been tested not only in a laboratory, but also in a real climbing situation.

CE is a European safety standard used for safety gear or Personal Protective Equipment — under which most climbing equipment is classified. The CE ISO 9002 stamp is a laboratory standard, albeit a very rigid one. An item with UIAA and CE markings has passed rigorous testing. All CE-rated pieces of equipment are supplied with comprehensive instructions and warnings about how they should (and should not) be used. Don't simply ignore these — a lot of useful information is supplied on those product instruction leaflets.

WHEN CHOOSING EQUIPMENT OR CLIMBING GEAR OF ANY KIND, LOOK OUT FOR THE STANDARD INTERNATIONAL SAFETY MARKINGS INDICATING THAT THE GEAR HAS BEEN PROPERLY TESTED.

Carabiners ('biners or crabs)

Also called snaplinks, these are used to attach climbers to ropes, belay devices, slings and protection placed in the rock. There are many variations, but essentially two main types: screwgate (locking) carabiners, and clipgate (snapgate) carabiners.

newton (N) is equivalent to about $\frac{1}{10}$kg of force (kgf), thus carabiners can effectively hold between 1000kgf to 4000kgf. This occurs along their major axis — if they are loaded sideways, with the gate open, then their strength is much less, it can be as low as 1000N (100kgf) to 7000N (700kgf).

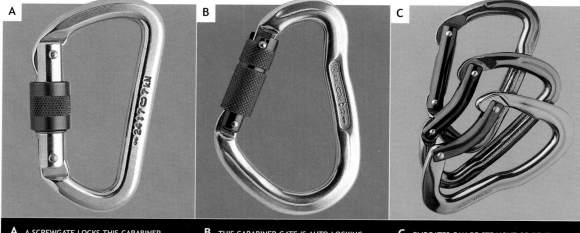

A A SCREWGATE LOCKS THIS CARABINER.   **B** THIS CARABINER GATE IS AUTO-LOCKING.   **C** CLIPGATES CAN BE STRAIGHT OR BENT.

Screwgate carabiners

To attach a rope to your harness, or for use anywhere where a single carabiner is used and should stay clipped, use a screwgate, or locking, carabiner. Some carabiners need to be screwed into position manually, whereas others are auto-locking.

Auto-locking carabiners

Auto-locking carabiners (or self-locking carabiners) are useful, as you cannot forget to lock the gate. Always keep the mechanism clean, however, otherwise it may not be able to auto-lock properly.

Clipgate (snapgate) carabiners

Clipgates are used to clip the rope into slings or pieces of protection. They are not as secure as locking gates, but easier to use if you have only one hand free.

Carabiner ratings

Carabiners are rated in kN (kiloNewton — a unit of force), the range usually being from 10kN to 40kN. One

SOME CARABINERS HAVE WIRE GATES IN PLACE OF SOLID GATES — THESE ARE ACTUALLY JUST AS STRONG AS NORMAL 'BINERS. THE WIRE GATE IS USED TO PREVENT 'WHIPLASH OPENING' OF THE GATE.

IN A FALL SITUATION, AS THE ROPE RACES OVER THE CARABINER, THE GATE CAN VIBRATE AND FLICK OPEN, POTENTIALLY ALLOWING THE ROPE TO JUMP OUT. A LIGHT WIRE GATE IS LESS LIKELY TO DO THIS, POSSIBLY MAKING IT SOMEWHAT SAFER TO USE.

Care of carabiners

To make them as light as possible, carabiners are made of alloys of aluminium. Unfortunately, this material is prone to chipping, cracking (if a carabiner is dropped) and damage by salt water.

Carabiners can be washed in soapy water, and then rinsed well. Drying with compressed air or even a hair-dryer works well. A bit of silicon spray on the gate will keep the action smooth. *(Never use oil, which can damage ropes, harnesses and nylon webbing.)*

⚠ Dropped equipment

Any carabiner or other piece of metal or plastic climbing gear which has been dropped from a height onto a hard surface must be treated as suspect, and preferably discarded. Invisible cracks and fractures can occur, which may cause collapse of the metal or plastic.

CARABINERS ARE THE KEY LINK BETWEEN CLIMBER AND PROTECTION.

⚠ Cross-loading of carabiners

The strength across the gate of a carabiner can be as low as 100kgf — so avoid this type of loading at all costs (see the photograph on the right). Always remember, also, to check any carabiner you use for the CE or UIAA stamp of approval — the Union Internationale des Associations d'Alpinisme is the world standards body for climbing equipment (see page 23). Certain makes of specialized, ultra lightweight carabiner do not carry the stamp of approval, and they may fail under load.

A WIDE VARIETY OF THESE devices is available, but they all serve the same function — to create friction as the rope passes over them, thus helping to slow the movement of the rope in the event of a fall, when a climber is being lowered or is rappelling. The stopping power — the force absorbed when held correctly by a moderately strong adult, before the rope begins to slide uncontrollably — is given as a kilogram-force range in brackets. The minimum is with thin smooth rope, the maximum with thick rough rope. There are four basic designs: Figure 8 (80–200kgf), Tube (200–400kgf), Plate (150–400kgf), and Grigri (200–350kgf); each of which has advantages and drawbacks.

Caution

Devices such as the Grigri have caused problems with unskilled users (pulling the lever back releases tension on the rope, thus lowering the climber). Serious accidents have been caused by belayers locking the device open instinctively or in panic as the climber starts to descend. Ensure your belayer is experienced in using a Grigri.

Name	Description	Advantages	Disadvantages
The Figure 8	■ These are the most commonly-used devices, especially amongst beginners and sport climbers. They are primarily used as descenders, but most of them can, at a push, be used for belaying (however not all of them, so check the instructions).	■ Inexpensive ■ Easy to load and use ■ Excellent for rappelling on single or double ropes ■ Can belay fairly efficiently on single rope. (Note: belaying with a Figure 8 is not highly recommended).	■ Not good for belaying on double ropes ■ Large and fairly heavy ■ Can twist ropes on belaying or during longish rappels ■ Very little friction, so probably not good for a novice belayer to use.
The Tube	■ This is a good buy, and very versatile — highly recommended. (The example shown is the popular DMM Bug.)	■ Relatively inexpensive ■ Lightweight ■ Can belay smoothly on single or double ropes ■ Can be used for rappelling ■ Generates a good deal of braking force ■ Can be attached to the harness with a short length of cord to prevent dropping.	■ Cannot be used for long, fast rappels as it heats up too much ■ Does not always give a smooth rappel.

Name	Description	Advantages	Disadvantages
Belay plate 	■ This is similar to the tube, but has different handling characteristics. The device can be loaded two ways, one gives less friction than the other for smoother belays and rappels, the other way holds larger falls.	■ Inexpensive ■ Easy to load and use ■ Good for rappelling on single or double ropes ■ Can belay efficiently on single or double ropes.	■ Cannot be used for long, fast rappels due to heat buildup ■ Gives a jerky rappel if ropes are wet or stiff.
Betterbrake 	■ A plate without a spring. When using for rappelling and in top-rope or sport belaying, where long leader falls are not expected, clip an extra 'biner between the plate and your own harness carabiner, for smoother action.	■ As above ■ A belay plate with a built-in spring (Sticht plate) gives smoother rope handling, especially when belaying or rappelling with double ropes.	■ As above ■ **NOTE**: Do **not** use this inserted carabiner method for situations where the leader can take a long fall, as it reduces the braking force by up to one-third.
Self-locking devices 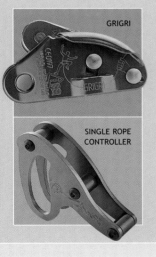 GRIGRI SINGLE ROPE CONTROLLER	■ These hold a falling climber without straining the hands, and also give additional safety in that an inattentive belayer won't drop a falling climber. They are popular with sport climbers, where short falls are common. These lock down when loaded, and take some (but not all!) of the responsibility from the belayer.	■ Lock automatically under load ■ Can be used to rappel ■ Prevent accidents resulting from belayer's inattention ■ Need very little hand strength to hold a fall, therefore they are useful with younger or inexperienced belayers ■ Will hold a fallen climber without straining the belayer's hand.	■ They are expensive — especially the Grigri ■ Heavy and bulky ■ Only work on single ropes, with a diameter of greater than 10mm (0.5in) ■ It is easy to make a potentially fatal mistake when loading the rope into these devices.

The rope

Once you get into real climbing, the rope is *the* most important piece of gear, and the common element in most types of climbing, bar the free solo forms. The rope is your safety line in case of a fall, your support when you are struggling with a difficult move, your way of getting back to the ground in many cases, and of getting up in others. Some climbers rope up for years without ever putting weight onto their ropes — but when they do need the rope, they need it big!

Climbing ropes are high-tech pieces of gear which should be chosen carefully and looked after lovingly. There is a lot of information here — but not too much! The chapter on Knowing the Ropes (page 32) will make you a much safer climber, so give it a good read.

Ropes come in two basic forms: *static* and *dynamic*, but both are of kernmantel construction.

Static versus dynamic ropes

Static ropes are ropes with little stretch, a tough outer sheath, and a rigid weave. They are usually used for caving (where ascenders are used), rappelling, as safety ropes on big peaks, or as haul ropes on big walls. Most static ropes are white, with colored

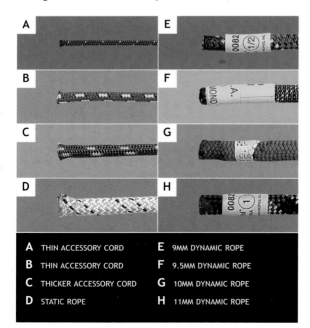

A	THIN ACCESSORY CORD	**E**	9MM DYNAMIC ROPE
B	THIN ACCESSORY CORD	**F**	9.5MM DYNAMIC ROPE
C	THICKER ACCESSORY CORD	**G**	10MM DYNAMIC ROPE
D	STATIC ROPE	**H**	11MM DYNAMIC ROPE

identification strips, although some are made in black or green — mostly for military purposes.

As their name suggests, *dynamic ropes* are 'movement' ropes. They have high energy absorption, as a result of their stretching capabilities of up to 30% — that is, a 50m (150ft) rope could let you fall an extra 15m (50ft) at full stretch! As ropes get older, their elasticity diminishes, and thus also their ability to hold falls.

Kernmantel rope construction

Kernmantel ropes have a braided core of fibres, surrounded by a woven sheath made of a slightly different material. Each minute fibre is continuous for the entire length of the rope. Ropes can be produced in different diameters, from a few millimetres to 20mm or more, and are available in any length, from metres to kilometres!

A MODERN KERNMANTLE ROPE HAS A COMPLEX INNER STRUCTURE.

The nature of the material, the diameter of the rope and the pattern of the weave create ropes with different handling properties, and differing degrees of strength, stretch and ruggedness. Most ropes are made of nylon, perlon, or some similar polyamide fibre.

The core (kern) is generally white (undyed) as dyeing can, albeit minutely, alter the strength of the filaments. The core accounts for up to 90% of the rope's strength. The outer sheath (mantle) is made in a wide variety of colors, both for rope identification, and to absorb damaging ultraviolet (UV) rays from the sun. The contrast of the sheath color against the white inner core also helps to show up abrasions or cuts in the rope.

Rope strength

The most vital function of the rope is to absorb energy resulting from a fall, or whilst rappelling. Ropes do this by stretching or twisting, right down to the molecular level. Kernmantel ropes can take great loads, from 10kN (1000kgf) in 8.5mm to 30kN (3000kgf) in 11mm. These are static loads, that is, the rope is gradually loaded until it breaks. In dynamic situations, when you are climbing, for instance, ropes experience shock-loading and whiplash, they pass over sharp edges and vibrate elastically whilst absorbing shock. This wear and tear reduces their actual breaking strength, sometimes drastically.

It is probably comforting to know, however, that very seldom do ropes break under normal use. After small falls, if you leave your rope unstressed for about half an hour, the rope slowly recovers and reverts to almost its original length and weave, although some of the tiny fibres may have broken. Allowing your rope to recover fully between falls will prolong its life span.

Buying a rope

Ropes are available in different diameters — the most usual being 9mm, 10.5mm or 11mm.

9mm ropes are classified (in terms of UIAA standards) as half ropes — that is, they are only considered safe if two ropes are used together. The '½' marking will appear on the rope end ferrules.

Double-rope climbing allows the leader to place protection away from the main line of the climb without causing undue friction, as he or she can clip one rope on one side, one more on the other. Two ropes also allow for longer rappels if used tied together.

10.5mm and 11mm ropes are classed as full ropes and marked '1' on the end ferrules. These are popular with sport climbers, or on climbs which do not vary much from a straight line.

Choose a rope

■ That suits your main type of climbing — two half ropes if you do mostly traditional climbing (see page 15), or a full rope if you do mostly sport climbing.

■ That is a good length — 50m (165ft) is the most common, although 60m (200ft) ropes are also popular.

■ That has handling properties you like — a balance has to be struck between suppleness, knotability and ease of coiling given by a looser sheath, and resistance to abrasion provided by a tight sheath.

■ That is water-resistant — especially if you do a lot of climbing in the wet or on snow or ice. Everdry-type ropes are coated with Teflon or silicone, which prevents water entering the weave and making the rope too heavy when it is wet.

⚠ Static ropes

Static ropes do not have high energy absorption, and are not safe for taking falls, such as you might take when leading, or even when longish falls (over 0.5m/1.5ft) are expected during top-roping. The ropes transmit forces of unacceptably high values to the protection pieces and the climber. *Never* use static ropes for leading — a fall on one could snap your neck!

A VARIETY OF DYNAMIC LEADING ROPES.

Care of your rope

Your rope is your lifeline — so treat it well. Avoid using it over sharp edges, as ropes cut disturbingly easily, especially when under load. Avoid long-term exposure to ultraviolet light (sunlight has plenty of this!) and don't leave it out in sunlight, or in the back window of your car. Chemicals are bad news, particularly strong acids (such as battery acid) or alkalis (such as from leaking torch batteries.) Sand and grit in the rope slowly cut the tiny fibres, so don't stand on it (or let your partner stand on it!). Ropes can and should be regularly washed in lukewarm water, with a mild soap. They can also be washed in a washing machine. Dry them in a cool place, or, if you're desperate, use the lowest heat setting in a tumble dryer.

A valuable purchase might be a rope bag; this useful piece of gear protects the rope from ultraviolet rays, sand, chemicals and abrasion.

A PROTECTIVE ROPE BAG IS A GOOD INVESTMENT.

A good rope bag

■ Opens out fully to provide easy access to the rope
■ Has solid fastening straps, and even some shoulder straps so that you can carry your rope easily
■ Has small tapes that you can tie your rope end to, to avoid tangles
■ Has an extra pouch for carrying boots, a chalk bag, quickdraws and other small odds and ends
■ Has a large groundsheet built into it, so that you can spread your rope out on it before climbing

Helmets

Many climbers sadly think that helmets are not 'cool', despite their obvious safety advantages. If you are sport climbing, this is fine, providing the rock is solid and your belayer (see page 42) is awake! In the case of trad climbing, however, wearing a helmet is a very good idea indeed, because falls are often longer and more serious than in sport climbing. The belayer can also be exposed to bits of loose rock and pieces of gear dropped from above.

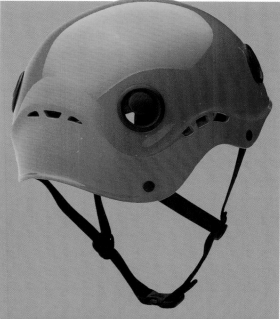

A GOOD CLIMBING HELMET, SUCH AS THIS LIGHTWEIGHT, VENTILATED CARBON-FIBRE VERSION, IS ESSENTIAL PROTECTION FOR TRAD CLIMBERS.

A good climbing helmet

■ Has a comfortable, well-fitting, adjustable head-band, which holds it solidly in place
■ Has a chin strap which buckles firmly, preventing the helmet from moving as your head moves
■ Has only a small front rim, to allow you to look up
■ Is light, without sacrificing strength
■ Is able to absorb some of the shock if you bang your head from the side
■ Has some form of ventilation

General care of equipment

Soft gear

Damage to soft gear is usually quite easy to spot. All ropes, harnesses, slings, tapes and webbing (usually made of nylon or polyamide) become damaged over time. Friction damage is usually clear, as items become visibly frayed, cut or melted. Soft gear which is badly discoloured (a sign of ultraviolet or chemical damage) or far more rigid or more supple than it originally was, should be retired. Soft gear must be retired after a major fall.

Hard gear

Metal equipment also degrades over time — and not only as a consequence of being nicked, chipped and dropped. Most modern hard gear is made of aluminium, which can alter its molecular structure with time and become brittle. This means that damage to hard gear is *not always visible* — so be careful.

All metal gear can be washed in cold or lukewarm, soapy water, and dried manually or left to dry in a cool, well-ventilated spot. Moving parts should be cleaned and lubricated with a silicone-based lubricant. *Never use oil-based lubricants, as these can damage nylon or polyester materials such as harnesses, ropes, tapes and slings that come into contact with the metal.*

When to retire your gear

Soft gear is usually given a life span of five years from the date of its first use, provided that it has never been subjected to 'poor conditions' during use or storage. Hard gear is given 10 years under ideal conditions. But this can all be academic — one really bad fall, or fuel from your benzine stove leaking out in your car boot, and the whole lot should be discarded. The golden rule is: Know Thy Gear. Keep track of the falls you take, and of how equipment has been treated. Bear in mind use during lending or borrowing.

Second-hand gear

With the high cost of new climbing equipment, you may be tempted to buy equipment second hand. Before buying any used climbing gear, make sure that you know its full history, and that you can trust the seller. Find out how and where the equipment was stored, why the owner wants to sell it, and how old it is. Your life — and someone else's — may depend on it!

Marking of gear

Most manufacturers recommend that no markings of any sort should be made on their items. What do you do, however, to prevent your gear becoming mixed up with that of other climbers,

or being lost or stolen? Usually it becomes necessary to use some identifying mark.

■ Avoid permanent marker pens or paints, as they contain solvents, which can damage soft gear, and their markings soon rub off hard gear.

■ Metal gear can be marked with paint, marker pens, or wrapped with coloured insulation tape or some similar material. Taped markings do not last all that long under the rigours of normal climbing use, but if the tape is regularly replaced, this is a good way of marking your hard gear in a highly visible way.

■ Although no manufacturer would dare to officially sanction this, careful *light* engraving of carabiners, descendeurs and other metal gear is tacitly accepted as non-damaging. Stamping of marks, or hard engraving on metal parts can damage their structure. Take care not to make marks on sections of metal over which the rope or other soft gear travels, as minute burrs in the metal can damage soft fibres.

■ Soft gear is best carefully marked using a highly visible marker pen on non-vital parts, not on load-bearing parts. Mark only the tips of ropes, the ends of harness straps, and use the manufacturers' marking tabs on slings, quickdraws and helmets.

Knowing the Ropes

most climbers make use of ropes, although, for a great deal of the time, the rope is not used actively. It is simply there — and you may even find it a nuisance. You drag it behind you when leading a climb, you climb with it above you for safety, it snags on every projection, and it always seems to get in the way. However, if something happens and you suddenly need the rope, you'll be extremely relieved to have it!

The most important thing to remember about tying on to the rope is that if you get it wrong, *someone could die*. Whichever knot you choose, you should be able to tie it when blindfolded, in a howling gale, or perched on a wobbling treetop. Practise tying this knot again and again — *before* you go anywhere near the rock face.

Knots for tying on to the rope

Any knot causes a loss of rope strength, as a result of the rope having to pass around itself on a small radius, and because of the internal friction in the knot if it is loaded (i.e. if it holds a fall or carries your body weight). Some knots lose a smaller percentage of rope strength than others (see page 36). In a major fall situation, this loss can be important. However, experience shows that it is *very* rare for the rope itself to break — far more often it is the points of attachment to the rock, slings or even the carabiners that give way. Any of the key knots discussed here can be considered safe if properly tied.

right A ROPE CAN MAKE THE DIFFERENCE BETWEEN LIFE AND DEATH.

Figure 8 on a Bight For tying rope to climbers or protection at any point in the rope

1	2	3
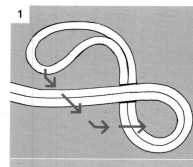		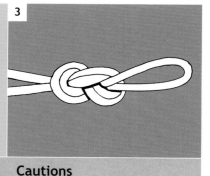

Advantages

■ The knot is quick to tie, and it is easy to see if it has gone wrong — the whole system is double looped
■ Even if undertied or overtied, it gives a safe knot — either a simple overhand, or a Figure 10
■ It can take load on any strand
■ It is a very strong knot, and loses little rope strength

Disadvantages

■ Can be difficult to untie after being loaded by body weight or a fall
■ It cannot be threaded through a harness loop
■ Difficult to adjust tightness or length

Cautions

Can work loose if tied at the end of a stiff, large-diameter rope. *Always* use an additional stopper knot

STOPPER KNOT: In Figure 8 and bowline knots, tie an overhand knot (see page 70), using the shorter end of the rope, around the other part of the rope, to lie against the main knot.

Figure 8 Re-threaded (Rewoven) For tying on to a harness or around a fixed point

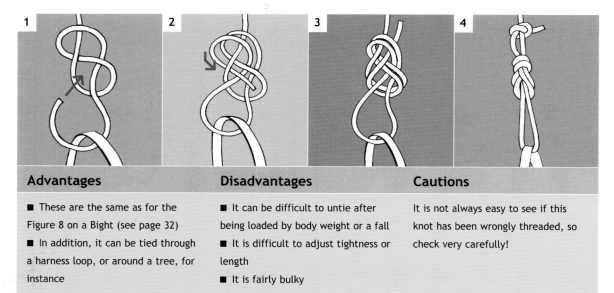

Advantages

■ These are the same as for the Figure 8 on a Bight (see page 32)
■ In addition, it can be tied through a harness loop, or around a tree, for instance

Disadvantages

■ It can be difficult to untie after being loaded by body weight or a fall
■ It is difficult to adjust tightness or length
■ It is fairly bulky

Cautions

It is not always easy to see if this knot has been wrongly threaded, so check very carefully!

Bowline For tying on to the rope or protection; or making a tie-in loop at the end of the rope for top-roping

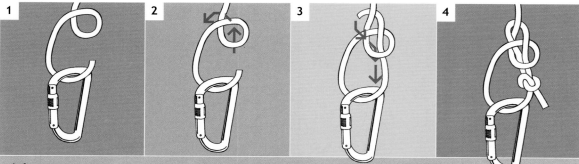

Advantages

■ It is less bulky than the Figure 8
■ It is easier to untie after being loaded
■ It is easy to adjust the length and tightness

Disadvantages

■ It is difficult to spot if this knot has been incorrectly tied
■ It does not take three-way loading well
■ It loses a greater percentage of rope strength than a Figure 8 knot
■ It is prone to working loose, so you should always tie a good stopper knot, preferably a double knot

Cautions

Single bowlines can, and do, work loose. It is also very easy to tie an incorrect version, which stays tied just long enough for a climber to get into trouble! Check very, very carefully each time you tie this knot, and always use a stopper knot.

Tape Sling The only truly safe knot to join two ends of climbing tape to form circular slings

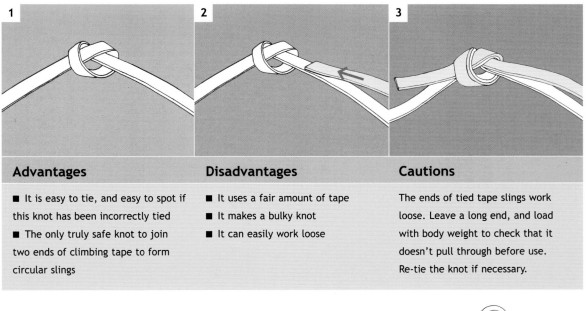

Advantages

■ It is easy to tie, and easy to spot if this knot has been incorrectly tied
■ The only truly safe knot to join two ends of climbing tape to form circular slings

Disadvantages

■ It uses a fair amount of tape
■ It makes a bulky knot
■ It can easily work loose

Cautions

The ends of tied tape slings work loose. Leave a long end, and load with body weight to check that it doesn't pull through before use. Re-tie the knot if necessary.

Clove Hitch To tie in to belay points where easy length adjustment is needed

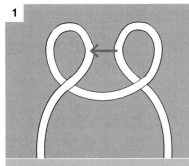
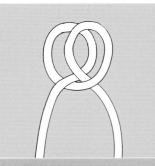
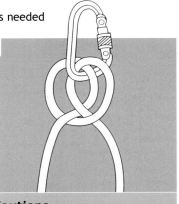

Advantages

■ It can be tied quickly and easily
■ It can be tied anywhere in the rope
■ It can take loads from both directions
■ It is easy to adjust the tension and position of the knot
■ It is easy to loosen after being loaded

Disadvantages

■ It can work loose
■ It loses a fair amount of rope strength

Cautions

Always tighten the Clove Hitch properly before use, otherwise it will 'run'.
Do not use a Clove Hitch as a main knot or as the only anchor knot.

Double Fisherman's Knot For joining two rope ends, for example, for long rappels

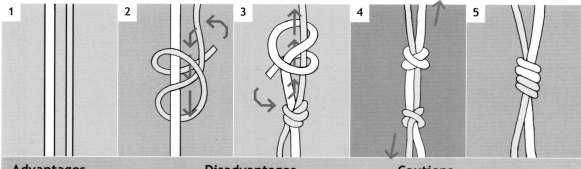

1 2 3 4 5

Advantages

- It does not easily work loose
- It is easy to spot if this knot has been incorrectly tied
- This knot can be used to join two rope ends, for example, to make a long rope for extended rappels

Disadvantages

- It requires a lot of rope — a length of at least eight times the diameter of the rope is necessary
- It is bulky
- It is quite difficult to untie after being loaded

Cautions

It is easy to get this knot the wrong way round. If it is not correctly tied, it is not as secure, and loses more rope strength.

Average knot strengths

Percentage of full, unknotted strength of rope or tape	
Figure 8	80%
Bowline	75%
Clove Hitch	65%
Tape Sling Knot	75%
Overhand Knot	65%
Double Fisherman's Knot	70%

⚠ Three elements of safety

There are three major considerations when using the rope to safeguard yourself and/or other climbers: tying on to it correctly, making sure that whatever it is attached to is absolutely secure, and using the correct belaying techniques (see page 40—43). Always bear these three elements in mind.

WHEN USED FOR BELAYING, ANCHORS (SEE OPPOSITE PAGE) SHOULD BE ABLE TO TAKE STRAIN IN ANY DIRECTION — UP, DOWN OR SIDEWAYS.

Tying on to the harness

For each type of harness there is a specific, safe way to tie on (some examples are shown below). If you are unsure of the procedure, consult the instructions supplied with it, or your supplier. In general, it is best to:
■ Keep the knot compact, fairly tight, and close to your body.
■ Tie a stopper knot in the end.
■ Keep the tail (outside the stopper knot) short.

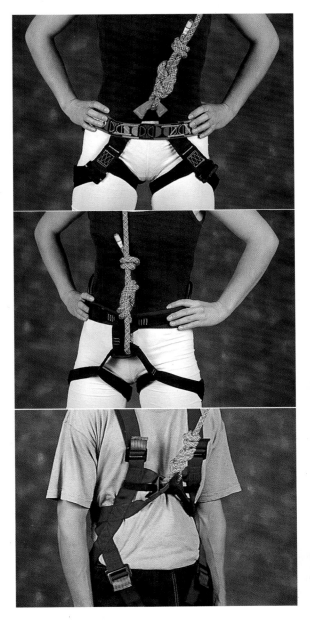

Attaching the rope to solid anchors

If you are climbing with friends, and using a rope, it is usual for the rope to be tied to two climbers — the climber and the belayer (see page 38) — as well as to one or more anchor or attachment points. Climbers often speak of the belay chain or the 'system' when referring to the climber, the rope, the belayer, and all the attachments to the rock or wall. In this instance, it is wise to remember the old saying that *a chain is only as strong as its weakest link*. Anchors must be solid, and so should the method of linking the rope to them.

Equalizing anchor points

This can be achieved by using slings (also called extensions), or by tying the rope via a Figure 8 on the Bight to the top, or furthest, protection point, and via one or more Clove Hitches to the other anchor points.

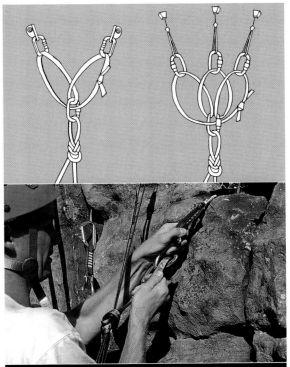

top EQUALIZING TWO- AND THREE-POINT ANCHORS USING ONE SLING.

above USING A KNOTTED SLING AS A CORDELETTE (SEE PAGE 38) TO EQUALIZE ANCHOR POINTS.

Setting up a cordelette

Another popular technique for tying on to an anchor point is to use a cordelette — this consists of 5 or 6m (18 to 20ft) of 7mm high-tensile cord tied into a large, open loop. You clip the loop into the protection points you want to use, pull the loops down to a common point, tie it all off with a Figure 8, and clip in. This is a safe and simple method, and ensures that all points are equally loaded. In addition, you don't waste your main rope, and the cordelette is light and compact.

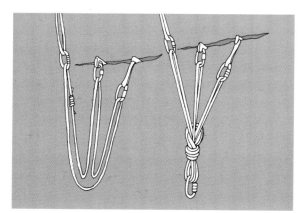

⚠ The dangerous triangle

As the angle between two anchor points increases, so does the load on each anchor. At angles close to 180°, it is dangerously high — keep the angle to a minimum by lengthening the tie-off if possible, or use two slings.

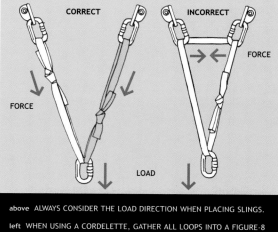

above ALWAYS CONSIDER THE LOAD DIRECTION WHEN PLACING SLINGS. left WHEN USING A CORDELETTE, GATHER ALL LOOPS INTO A FIGURE-8 KNOT ON A BIGHT, ENSURING THE TENSION IS EQUAL ON ALL POINTS.

The climbing system A Multi-pitch Climb

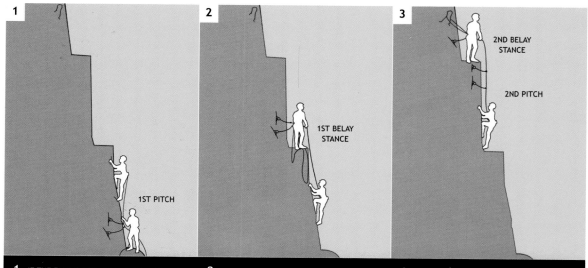

1 IF THE FACE IS TOO HIGH TO BE CLIMBED ON A SINGLE ROPE, THE ROUTE IS BROKEN INTO PITCHES. THE LEADER CLIMBS THE FIRST PITCH.

2 WHEN THE LEADER REACHES A SUITABLE LEDGE, HE/SHE SETS UP ANCHOR POINTS AND BELAYS THE SECOND CLIMBER TO THE LEDGE.

3 THE LEADER THEN CONTINUES TO THE SECOND BELAY STANCE, PLACING PROTECTION WHICH IS REMOVED BY THE SECOND CLIMBER.

Climbing calls or 'commands'

Leader	Second
On placing a runner: **'Runner in, climbing'**	**'Climb'**
On reaching the top of the pitch, organizing a belay and clipping into it: **'Off belay'**	Takes leader off belay: **'Belay off'**
Leader takes in rope until it comes tight on the second	**'That's me'**
Leader places the second on belay, and checks all anchors: **'Climb when you're ready'** or just **'Climb'**	Removes any anchors, checks knots, etc.: **'Climbing'**
'Climb' or 'OK'	

If, during the second's climb, various actions need to take place, the usual communications are:

Leader	Second
	Slack rope is needed (for instance, to climb back down a little, or to take out a piece of protection gear: **'Slack'**
Leader slacks rope	
	Tight rope is needed for security, or to hang on in order to retrieve a piece of protection gear: **'Tight rope'**
Leader pulls in rope	
To indicate a falling rock or other object	**'Below!'** (this call can be made by either climber).

CALLS BETWEEN CLIMBERS SHOULD BE SHORT, SIMPLE AND EASILY UNDERSTOOD BY BOTH CLIMBERS, ESPECIALLY IN SITUATIONS WHERE THE LEADER AND SECOND ARE NOT VISIBLE TO EACH OTHER.

Belaying

THE TERM BELAYING REFERS TO the process of holding and managing the rope in such a way that you safeguard your fellow climber. If your partner should fall while you are belaying, your role is to limit the distance of the fall, usually by using one of a number of friction-enhancing devices on the rope. As when tying knots, you may literally have your partner's life in your hands, as you can prevent him or her from hitting the ground.

Belay devices

Most climbers use some form of belay device so that they are able to increase or decrease the amount of friction applied to the rope. Most belay devices allow for rappelling or descending (see page 70) as well as belaying. There are four basic designs: the Figure 8, the Plate, the Tube and the Self-locking devices (see right, and pages 26-27).

Each device has advantages and disadvantages; each has its proponents. All work well with single ropes, but only the Tubes and Plates allow for the use of double ropes (see pages 26–27).

All the belay devices work on the principle of dynamic (planned) rope slippage after a certain amount of braking force has been supplied. This helps to dissipate or absorb the high energy or force generated by the fall. The force can be as high as 4kN (400kgf), that is, the belay device will not allow any major rope slippage until the fall force exceeds 400kgf (assuming that the rope is firmly held by a reasonably strong person). After this point, the rope begins to move rapidly through the system, and also through the belayer's hand.

A WELL-ORGANIZED HANGING BELAY. NOTE THE MULTIPLE PROTECTION POINTS, EARLY LEADER PROTECTION AND CAREFUL ROPE MANAGEMENT TO AVOID SNAGGING.

Friction Hitch Used with a carabiner for belaying

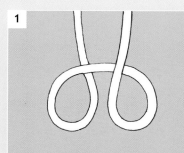

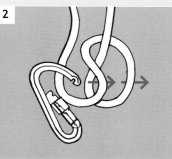

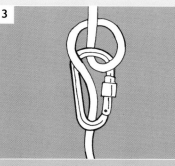

Advantages

- The knot has a braking force of up to 300kgf
- It is easy to tie
- It can be tested for correctness before being loaded
- It can be made in single or double ropes

Disadvantages

- It twists the rope
- The friction of rope-on-rope can wear the rope rapidly

Cautions

The Friction Hitch (also called a Munter or Italian Hitch) easily unlocks screwgate carabiners if the rope runs across the gate. Always load the carabiner in the correct way (see page 24–25).

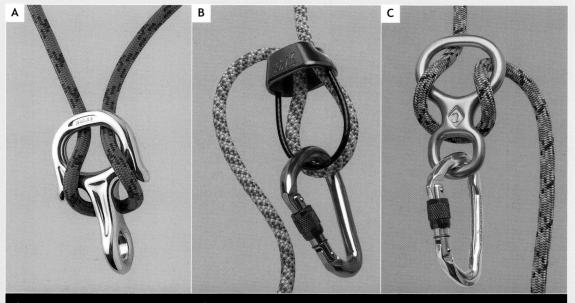

A THIS BAD BRAKING POSITION WITH A FIG. 8 DESCENDEUR GIVES TOO LITTLE FRICTION.

B A BELAY TUBE OR PLATE CAN BE USED WITH SINGLE OR DOUBLE ROPES.

C A FIGURE 8 CORRECTLY POSITIONED FOR BELAYING. (NOTE CAUTIONS ON PAGE 26).

BELAYING IS BOTH A SCIENCE and an art — a good, attentive, thoughtful belayer not only makes it safer for the climber, but can also make the climber's task easier. By careful positioning of the rope, the belayer and the rest of the system, the rope can be allowed to flow freely to the climber. The belayer can give slack exactly when the leader or climber needs it, or tighten the rope for security or to assist a struggling climber.

Direct and indirect belays

The belay device can be attached directly to the anchor(s), or the belayer can tie on, then attach the belay to him or herself. If the belay is a direct belay, then the anchors must be 'bomb-proof', as any forces come directly onto these. Usually, belays are indirect. The belayer's body absorbs some of the force, thus loading the anchors less than in the direct belay. The disadvantage is that the belayer

might be subjected to quite a shock, and can be pulled around by a fall.

Anchors

Anchors should be set to anticipate any likely direction of pull. Take special care if you are belaying below an overhang — many a belayer has received a crack on the skull by being pulled up into an overhanging rock!

The carabiner(s) used to clip in to the final belay or anchor point should be screwgate (locking) carabiners (see page 24). If these are not available, use two clip-gate (snapgate) carabiners (see page 24) with their gates reversed, to prevent accidental opening as far as possible.

Belaying from below

If you are belaying from the ground, remember that the pull in case of a fall will be upward. If you are belaying on a ledge halfway up a route, the pull could be upward, or downward if the leader falls before placing his or her first runner. Always place anchors so that they can cater for both these directions (see page 37—38).

Belaying from above

If you are belaying from above the climber, the direction of pull in the case of a fall is downward. The belayer (often the leader)

A A DIRECT BELAY AVOIDS PLACING LOAD ON THE BELAYER, BUT MUST HAVE AN ABSOLUTELY 'BOMB-PROOF' SET OF ANCHORS.
B INDIRECT BELAYS PLACE THE BODY OF THE BELAYER INTO THE BELAY CHAIN, PLACING LESS STRESS ONTO THE ANCHORS, BUT MAKING IT DIFFICULT FOR THE BELAYER TO ESCAPE THE SYSTEM IF NECESSARY.

THIS BELAYER HAS BOTH HANDS CORRECTLY PLACED TO ARREST A FALL.

■ Ensure that the belay hand is free to move fully into the braking position (see left) — avoid being too close up to the rock face, for instance.

■ Set up the belay so that the belayer faces the direction in which the leader or climber will be moving.

■ Always tie the free end of the rope to the belayer, or to a solid anchor. At the very least, tie a knot in it. This is extremely important in multi-pitch climbs (see page 38), and can even be vital in ground belaying on single-pitch routes — the climb may be 30m (100ft) and your rope only 45m (150ft). Should the leader or climber fall off at or near the top, he or she may fall 30m x 2 = 60m (200ft) — further than the length of your rope! Many a climber has hit the ground — and sometimes with tragic results — as a result of the rope end passing through the belay device.

■ Communicate — the belayer and leader should each always know what the other person has in mind. When the leader reaches the top of a pitch, it is vital for the belayer to know what the climber's intentions are — will he or she be lowering off, rappeling, or bringing the belayer up and continuing on another pitch? (See also Climbing Calls on page 39).

must ensure that the rope does not pass across his body in such a way that it traps legs or arms. By placing himself 'in the system', the belayer reduces the strain on the anchors, but increases the strain on himself.

A few essentials

■ Always ensure that the rope will be able to run freely — the best method is for the belayer to tie on to an end, then loosely coil the rest of the rope on the ground until the leader's end of the rope lies freely on the top. This procedure should be followed not only at ground level, but at each stance on a multi-pitch climb.

THE BELAYER HAS ALLOWED THE ROPE TO TRAP HIS LEG AS THE CLIMBER FALLS. THIS CAN BE BOTH PAINFUL AND DANGEROUS IF HE HAS TO ESCAPE THE SYSTEM FOR ANY REASON.

Climbing Techniques

Climbing is all about movement — the more fluid and relaxed you are, the easier you will find it. Like other sports, it calls for certain patterns of movement — called engrams — to be learnt and practised. Engrams also form the basis of dancing, athletics and the martial arts, for example. The common element is that of establishing patterns of movement, which the body refers to automatically. The following need to be combined:

Technique — the efficient use of energy by means of balance and body positioning, and by using only the necessary muscle groups for any one move or set of moves in a pattern.

The mind game — being relaxed and confident about your climbing, and recognizing and making the most of your talents.

Power and strength — qualities that can be developed with time and effort.

VARIOUS SPORTS REQUIRE YOU TO DEVELOP ENGRAMS, OR PATTERNS OF MOVEMENT (LEFT). ONCE YOU HAVE LEARNED THE BASIC CLIMBING ENGRAMS (RIGHT), YOUR CLIMBING WILL BECOME MORE RELAXED AND FLUID AND YOU WILL DEVELOP MORE CONFIDENCE.

MOST CLIMBING MOVEMENT STEMS from the feet and legs, not the hands (try going up a flight of steps on your hands!). By keeping the weight over the feet as much as possible, the climber gains advantage. Leaning too far into the rock reduces the grip on the feet, and leaning too far out has the same effect. Even under overhangs, clever use of the feet can take load off the arms.

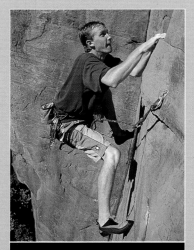

FRICTION: SLABS ARE BEST CLIMBED BY SMEARING — KEEPING THE LARGEST POSSIBLE AREA IN CONTACT WITH THE ROCK.

FRONT POINTING: THE TOE CAN BE USED ON TINY EDGES, OR FORCED INTO MINUSCULE POCKETS IN THE ROCK.

HEEL HOOKS: THIS IS A VALUABLE WAY TO TAKE THE WEIGHT OFF THE ARMS.

EDGING: SMALL PROTRUSIONS CAN BE STOOD ON BY USING BOTH THE INSIDE AND OUTSIDE EDGES OF THE BOOT.

TOE HOOK: THIS TECHNIQUE IS LARGELY USED TO MAINTAIN THE CLIMBER'S BALANCE, AND SELDOM TO MOVE UPWARD, ALTHOUGH IT CAN TAKE WEIGHT OFF THE CLIMBER'S HANDS.

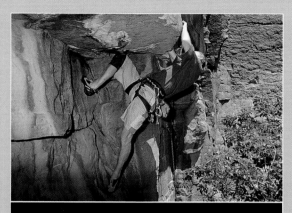

KNEE-BARS: THESE ARE VALUABLE FOR RESTS OR WHEN CLIPPING GEAR.

DROP-KNEE: THIS TECHNIQUE GIVES OPPOSING FORCES ON THE CLIMBER'S FEET, MAKING FULL USE OF TINY SIDEWAYS PROTRUSIONS.

FLAGGING: THIS IS USED TO HELP THE CLIMBER BALANCE RATHER THAN TO CONTRIBUTE TO UPWARD MOVEMENT.

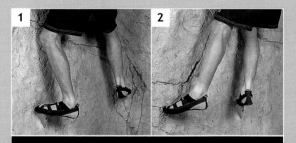

FOOT SWITCHES: THE SAME HOLD, USED FIRST BY ONE FOOT, AND THEN THE OTHER, ALLOWS YOU TO CHANGE THE DIRECTION OF MOVEMENT, OR TO MOVE ONE FOOT FURTHER ALONG WHEN TRAVERSING.

STEMMING (BRIDGING): THIS IS ANOTHER TECHNIQUE THAT ALLOWS CLIMBERS TO REST OR TO GET SUPPORT FOR UPWARD MOVES FROM MINUTE HOLDS, OFTEN IN AN OPEN-BOOK CRACK SUCH AS THIS.

Hand techniques

THE HANDS ARE FAR MORE AGILE and mobile than the feet. The ability of our fingers to spread apart, to curl and to fold, to pinch and to squeeze, gives rise to a vast variety of possible combinations — almost as diverse as the range of possible holds!

Some of the techniques shown here may have to be combined to produce the desired result of allowing you to 'stick' to the rock.

PINCH GRIPS: SOME HOLDS ALLOW FOR THIS, WHICH CAN BE PREFERABLE TO SIDE-PULLING OR CRIMPING.

THE OPEN HAND: IT IS MORE TENDON-FRIENDLY, BUT OFTEN LESS POSITIVE. IT IS MORE USEFUL ON LARGER HOLDS.

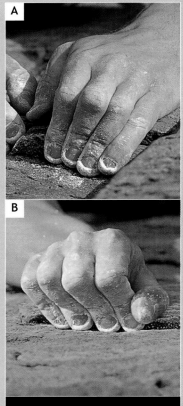

A

B

SIDE-PULLS: THIS HOLD CAN BE MAXIMIZED BY LEANING THE BODY SIDEWAYS AWAY FROM THE GRIP.

UNDERCLINGS: OFTEN NEGLECTED, THIS IS A MOST USEFUL WAY TO MOVE UPWARD. IT IS BEST TO GET YOUR FEET HIGH.

THE CRIMP: HERE THE FINGERS ARE BENT TO TAKE HOLD OF A SMALL EDGE. THE GRIP IS STRENGTHENED IF YOU FOLD YOUR THUMB OVER SOME OF THE FINGERS, BUT THIS IS HARD ON THE TENDONS. THERE ARE CLOSED CRIMPS (SEE **A**), WHERE THE FINGERS ARE BENT OVER AND OPEN CRIMPS, WHERE THE FINGERS ARE FOLDED IN (SEE **B**). THESE STRESS TENDONS IN A DIFFERENT WAY — EXPERIMENT AND SEE WHICH WORKS BEST FOR YOU IN A PARTICULAR SITUATION.

Jamming

Hand and finger jams can be painful, but they are often the best or the only way to tackle rock with vertical or horizontal cracks. Hand jams can be divided into *fist jams* and *palm* or *hand* jams. To use the jamming technique successfully, you need to strike a delicate balance between too much effort — a waste of energy leading to crunched knuckles — and too little effort — leading to shredded skin and a fall as the jam comes adrift.

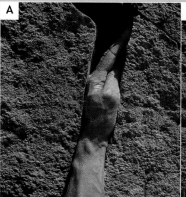

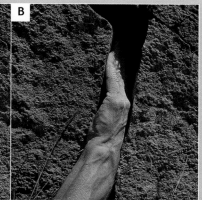

PALM JAMS (HAND JAMS): BY CUPPING YOUR PALM AS YOU INSERT YOUR HAND INTO A CRACK, YOU CAN EXERT GREATER FORCE. USE YOUR THUMB WHERE IT WORKS BEST, EITHER INSIDE OR OUTSIDE THE FINGERS. YOU CAN INSERT THE HAND 'THUMB UP' OR 'THUMB DOWN'. THE THUMB DOWN POSITION, WHICH FEELS QUITE AWKWARD, IS THE MOST SECURE.

FIST JAMS: A CLENCHED FIST, WITH THE THUMB EITHER ON THE INSIDE OR OUTSIDE, CAN GIVE A SOLID GRIP IN A CRACK OF THE RIGHT WIDTH. BEING TENTATIVE ABOUT A JAM ONLY CAUSES MORE PAIN — SO POSITION YOUR FIST AND SQUEEZE LIKE CRAZY TO ENSURE A SECURE FIT.

STACKING YOUR FINGERS, OR PLACING SEVERAL FINGERS ONE ABOVE THE OTHER IN A SMALL POCKET IN A VERTICAL CRACK, CAN ALSO GIVE A SECURE GRIP.

FINGER JAMS (FINGER LOCKS): FOR THIS KIND OF JAM, FINGERS — FROM JUST THE FINGERTIPS OF TWO FINGERS TO THE FULL EXTENT OF ALL THE FINGERS — MAY BE FITTED INTO A CRACK, AND TWISTED TO TIGHTEN THE FIT, IF NECESSARY.

OFTEN USING THE THUMB AGAINST THE EDGE OF THE CRACK ENHANCES THE GRIP. HANDS CAN BE 'SHUFFLED' UP, OR CROSSED OVER PAST ONE ANOTHER.

Taping fingers and hands

In order to succeed in hand and finger jams, without shredding the skin too much, many climbers tape up either the finger joints (finger jams) or the hand, particularly the back (hand jams). A non-elastic (surgical) tape is best for the task.

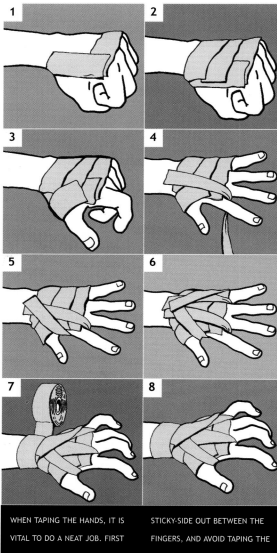

WHEN TAPING THE HANDS, IT IS VITAL TO DO A NEAT JOB. FIRST DRY THE HANDS THOROUGHLY, AND ENSURE THE TAPE ADHERES PROPERLY AT EACH STAGE. LAYER TAPE OVER THE BACK OF THE HAND, FOLD NON-ELASTIC TAPE STICKY-SIDE OUT BETWEEN THE FINGERS, AND AVOID TAPING THE PALM OF THE HAND.
AN ADDITIONAL BAND AROUND THE WRIST AND LOWER HAND MAY BE NECESSARY TO ENSURE THAT THE TAPE STAYS IN PLACE.

REALLY WIDE CRACKS CALL FOR UNUSUAL TECHNIQUES. CLIMBERS MAY NEED TO SHUFFLE THE WHOLE BODY INTO 'OFF-WIDTH' CRACKS; USE ARM BARS (**A**); CHICKENWINGS (PALMS AGAINST ONE SIDE OF THE ROCK, ELBOWS AND BACK AGAINST THE OTHER); OR T-BARS FOR FEET (**B**).

Some combined techniques

Although hand and foot techniques can be discussed separately for convenience and clarity, they are mostly used in conjunction to achieve the final result. Try to combine the movements of the hands and feet in your imagination as you study the pictures.

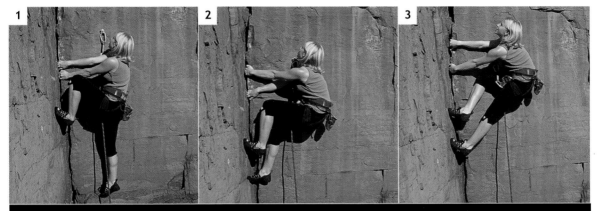

LAY-BACKS: HERE THE HANDS ARE SIDE-PULLING, AND THE FEET ARE EITHER PUSHING AGAINST ONE EDGE OF THE CRACK OR USUALLY FLAT OR SMEARING ON SOME OTHER SURFACE. LAY-BACK TECHNIQUES ARE OFTEN USED IN CORNERS OR CRACKS. AVOID PLACING THE FEET TOO HIGH IN A CRACK, AS THIS PUTS MORE STRAIN ONTO THE ARMS. RATHER USE A SERIES OF SHORT FOOT AND HAND MOVES TO GAIN HEIGHT. ESTABLISHING A GOOD RHYTHM IS IMPORTANT, AS IT HELPS FLUIDITY OF MOVEMENT AND IT SAVES ENERGY. LAY-BACKING TECHNIQUES CAN BE VERY TIRING, AND ONCE AGAIN, A GOOD RHYTHM HELPS, IF THE CRACK ALLOWS IT. ONCE IN A LAY-BACK, IT IS DIFFICULT TO GET OUT OF IT, SO ENSURE THAT YOU HAVE ENOUGH ENERGY IN RESERVE TO GET TO THE REST POINT YOU'RE AIMING FOR!

MANTLE SHELVES: THIS, AS THE NAME SUGGESTS, IS A TECHNIQUE FOR GETTING UP ONTO A SMALL PLATFORM. YOU PUSH UP WITH AN ARM AND SHOULDER, WITH YOUR FEET OFTEN 'TAPPING' UP THE WALL LITTLE BY LITTLE UNTIL ONE OR BOTH END UP NEAR YOUR HANDS. OFTEN THERE IS NO GOOD HAND-HOLD ABOVE THE SHELF — SO CAREFUL ATTENTION TO BALANCE IS VITAL!

STEMMING (BRIDGING): THIS INVOLVES BOTH HANDS AND FEET, AND CAN BE A USEFUL REST TECHNIQUE AS WELL AS A CLIMBING TOOL.

CHIMNEYING: THERE ARE NUMEROUS WAYS TO CHIMNEY, THE LEAST STRENUOUS BEING THE CLASSIC CHIMNEY, WHERE THE FEET GIVE MOST OF THE UPWARD MOVEMENT. BY ALTERNATING THE FOOT WHICH DOES THE PUSHING, YOU CAN AVOID STRESSING ONLY ONE KNEE.

BODY TWISTS (TWISTLOCKS): IN THIS MANOEUVRE, TURN THE UPPER BODY SO THAT THE ARM CLOSEST TO THE ROCK 'LOCKS OFF' THAT IS, GIVES THE OTHER (OUTER) ARM MAXIMUM EXTENSION ABILITY.

CHIMNEYING: FOR WIDE CHIMNEYS, ONE SOMETIMES NEEDS TO USE A BRIDGE METHOD (ALSO CALLED BACK AND FOOTING). THIS CAN BE VERY STRENUOUS, AS YOU EXERT FORCE OUTWARDS ONTO EACH WALL.

CLIMBERS TALK ABOUT THE 'flow' — suddenly everything comes together, and your body just flows up the rock. There is no easy explanation for why this suddenly happens one day, and on another, you feel like a clumsy Godzilla. Frequently, climbers cannot actually remember details of a fluid climb — it 'just happens'. One of the world's most consistent climbers, Catherine Destivelle, states that one can train for this 'flow'. She attributes her performance to striving for a rhythm — she imagines herself dancing up the rock, looking only to her pattern of steps. This vizualization is undoubtedly an important part of climbing, the ability to free your mind from the cares of the world, the day, the climb, and focus only on the next few instants.

It is easy to forget to rest, and, more importantly, to breathe properly. Most climbing is aerobic, that is, it is done slowly enough for the energy we need to be generated by burning (metabolizing) the food in our bodies in the presence of oxygen. Sometimes it passes into the anaerobic phase, when we burn energy too fast for our bodies to supply oxygen to the muscle fibres, and the stored food has to be burned via another process, which occurs without oxygen. This process is less efficient, and creates lactic acid as a waste product. This collects in the muscles, slowing them down (being 'pumped' is the normal climbers' term for this) and eventually causing stiffness or a cramp. In tense climbing situations, climbers can virtually forget to breathe, hastening the advent of the anaerobic phase. Be aware of your breathing — keep it deep, and regular.

Resting

Resting, too, is vital — it allows you to catch up on breathing, to 'shake out' your muscles (jacking up your blood supply, and removing wastes as well as providing new oxygen and food) and to examine the route ahead. It also allows you to chalk up your fingers or hands — often essential on slippery or smooth rock, or just to dry those sweaty palms. Chalking up at just the right time can make all of the difference.

Rest on a straight arm if possible (see left), to reduce muscle tension. By making use of knee bars, stems (bridges), drop-knees, heel hooks, constant hand-swaps, or a combination of these, you can take the weight off your arms. Constantly be on the lookout for rests, however marginal they may be.

SLOW, CALCULATED, CALM AND PRECISE MOVEMENTS CHARACTERIZE THE BEST CLIMBERS, WHO MAKE CLIMBING LOOK SO EASY. THIS CLIMBER IS RESTING A LITTLE ON A STRAIGHT ARM.

Leading a Climb

being sufficiently skilled to lead a climb is probably the ultimate aim of most climbers. Instead of following someone else's lead, you can plan and execute your own climb, in your own way, in your own time — just you, your partner(s) and the rock. Leading can be done in two ways: by using fixed gear, such as pre-placed, solid bolts and pegs; or by using natural or trad gear, namely gear that the leader places into rock cracks or fissures while climbing the route. The latter constitutes the sharp end of the sport and, as such, it presents the biggest challenge, and the most danger. Using pre-placed gear is the accepted way of sport climbing. Although this is potentially less dangerous, it is no less strenuous, nor less demanding, of technique than trad climbing.

Leading for the first time

There are a number of ways in which you can make your first attempts at leading easier:

■ Be less ambitious to begin with, and start leading on routes with much lower grades (see page 92) than those you normally follow or top-rope.

■ On routes that are new to you, ask people who have done the climb where the problem areas are, and how best to overcome them.

■ Plan your moves before you begin: study the route, and decide how you are going to tackle it, bearing in mind which piece of protection gear you will place where, when, and how. Even if you only succeed in following your plan for the first few metres (or feet), seeing your moves working will boost your confidence.

■ For longer pitches or even multi-pitch routes, break the climb down into manageable sections — the psychological advantage of facing a few manageable sections rather than one long, amorphous horror will help a good deal.

■ Take time to organize your gear properly before you begin — rack your quickdraws and/or protection pieces carefully, in an order that you know, to avoid fumbling and consequent loss of strength and confidence.

■ Explain to your belayer exactly what your plan is, for instance, when you are likely to want slack, and make sure that you agree on a clear system of communication signals (see page 39).

above A LEADER HAS A RESPONSIBILITY TO HIS, OR HER, PARTY TO PROVIDE SAFE LEADING AND GOOD BELAYING.

right THE EXPERIENCE OF LEADING IS VERY DIFFERENT TO SECONDING OR TOP-ROPING. ON LEAD, THE PITCH THAT YOU FLOATED UP ON TOP-ROPE SEEMS TO HAVE LOST HALF ITS HOLDS AND BECOME TWICE AS STEEP. THE 'ROCK DEVILS' OF FEAR HAVE GRABBED YOU, ADDING KILOGRAMS OF DOUBT TO YOUR LOAD, WEAKENING YOUR MUSCLES AND CLOUDING YOUR MIND. HERE, FRENCH CLIMBER CATHERINE DESTIVELLE, SHOWS THE BENEFIT OF HER YEARS OF CLIMBING IN HER RELAXED, ELEGANT STYLE.

Leading sport routes

Sport (or bolted) routes are not necessarily limited to single-pitch climbs — there are many routes in France, Italy, Spain, America and elsewhere which are technically sport routes, relying on bolted gear only, and which are many pitches long. If you are attempting any of these, make sure that most of the techniques used in leading traditional routes — such as what to do on intermediate stances on a multi-pitch climb (page 38), rappelling (abseiling) off (pages 68–71), and rescue skills (pages 74–75) — are part of your repertoire.

IN SPORT CLIMBS, THE QUICKDRAW IS THE MAIN TOOL. THIS CONSISTS OF TWO SNAPGATE CARABINERS JOINED BY A SHORTISH PIECE OF TAPE SLING. THE TWO CARABINERS ARE USUALLY POSITIONED WITH THEIR GATES FACING IN OPPOSITE DIRECTIONS, AS THIS MAKES IT EASIER TO CLIP THE ROPE IN CORRECTLY.

LEADING A TRIED AND TESTED SPORT ROUTE IS ONE OF THE MOST SATISFYING THINGS YOU CAN DO — CLIMBING, CLIPPING, AND CLIMBING FURTHER. IF YOU FALL, YOU HAVE THE SECURITY OF GOOD, SOLID BOLTS PLACED BY AN EXPERT TO CATCH YOU. IF YOU ARE CLIMBING A ROUTE YOU DON'T KNOW, HOWEVER, DON'T MAKE THE MISTAKE OF ASSUMING THAT EVERY PIECE OF PROTECTION GEAR YOU COME ACROSS IS SECURE — ALWAYS TEST IT FIRST.

ARRANGE THESE QUICKDRAWS ON YOUR HARNESS GEAR LOOPS, WITH A FEW ON EACH SIDE — YOU MIGHT NEED TO CLIP THE HANGER AND/OR THE ROPE WITH EITHER HAND (IT IS WELL WORTH PRACTISING THIS).

Clipping skills

On quickdraws, climbers usually use one straight-gate carabiner, which is used to clip the bolt hanger, and one bent-gate carabiner, into which the rope is clipped. This arrangement has the advantage of enabling you to easily identify which carabiner should go into the hanger — this carabiner will get chipped and burred by the metal hangers, and could damage the rope, so check it regularly. The bent gate allows for easier location and clipping in of the rope — an important factor when a fraction of a second could make the difference between your completing the move or falling off.

When clipping, ensure that the rope follows the anticipated direction of travel, and is clipped in from behind the quickdraw (against the rock). It should not go across the gate, where it could unclip itself.

When clipping the rope, warn your belayer (for instance, by shouting 'Clipping' or 'Slack') so that he or she can give you the slack you need. Pull up just enough rope (experience will help here!) and clip with your free hand. If you are able to, clip whilst on a rest, or with your holding arm straight, as this uses less energy.

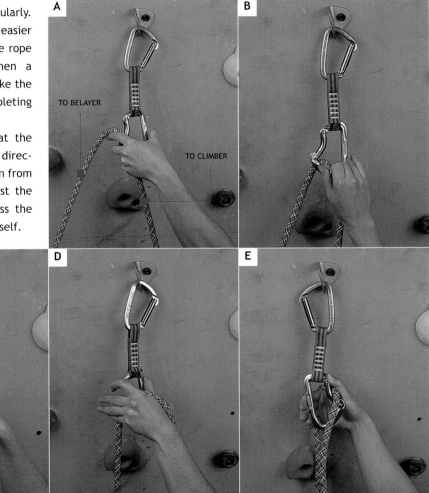

THERE ARE MANY WAYS TO CLIP THE QUICK-DRAW RAPIDLY. PRACTISE DOING THEM WITH BOTH HANDS, AND CHOOSE YOUR FAVOURITE FOR EACH SITUATION. IN ALL CASES, THE ROPE TO THE CLIMBER'S HARNESS MUST LIE IN FRONT OF THE CARABINER, WHILE THE ROPE TO THE BELAYER LIES AGAINST THE ROCK.

A A SPREAD HAND STABILIZES THE 'BINER, WITH THE FINGERS CLIPPING.

B THE MIDDLE FINGER PULLS DOWN, STABILIZING THE 'BINER AND THE FOREFINGER AND THUMB CLIP.

C THE BACK (SPINE) OF THE CARABINER IS HELD BETWEEN TWO FINGERS.

D THE WHOLE HAND STABILIZES THE CARABINER, WHILE THE THUMB ONLY CLIPS.

E A DIFFERENT WAY OF STABILIZING THE CARABINER WITH THE FINGERS.

Topping out (lowering off)

As said previously, most sport routes — although not all of them — are a single pitch long, and it is usual for the leader to be lowered off by the belayer. Some routes have convenient, neat *in situ* carabiners at the top, and you can just clip in, and ask to be lowered. Most routes don't have this, however. To avoid leaving gear behind, you have to untie from your rope, thread it through chains or shackles, tie on again, and then lower off. This process can be hazardous if you don't have the sequence down pat, so carefully study the illustrations and instructions on this and the following page.

1 ON ARRIVING AT THE TOP BELAY POINT(S), CLIP IN TWO QUICKDRAWS, AND CLIP ON TO EACH BOLT INDEPENDENTLY.

2 IT IS OFTEN WISE TO CLIP THE FIRST BOLT, THEN CLIP YOUR ROPE INTO THIS QUICKDRAW BEFORE CLIPPING THE SECOND QUICKDRAW DIRECTLY INTO YOUR HARNESS ATTACHMENT (TIE-IN) LOOP(S). (REMEMBER, YOU WILL BE TIRED, AND YOU COULD FALL OFF WHILE TRYING TO CLIP YOUR HARNESS TO THE QUICKDRAWS.) RECLIP THE FIRST QUICKDRAW ALSO DIRECTLY INTO YOUR HARNESS.

3 HANG ON THESE, CALL FOR SLACK, TIE A FIGURE 8 ON THE BIGHT WELL BELOW YOUR BODY. PULL THIS UP, AND CLIP IT TO A CARABINER ON YOUR HARNESS TIE-IN POINT. THIS IS A BACK-UP IN CASE ANYTHING GOES WRONG WITH THE QUICKDRAWS.

4 NOW UNTIE, THREAD THE ROPE THROUGH THE BOTTOM CHAINS, OR THE SHACKLES, AND TIE BACK IN. DOUBLE CHECK EVERYTHING.

5 UNTIE THE FIGURE 8 ON THE BIGHT, AND ASK YOUR BELAYER TO TIGHTEN THE ROPE ON YOU. CHECK AGAIN, THEN UNCLIP THE QUICKDRAWS.

6 YOUR BELAYER CAN NOW CAREFULLY LOWER YOU TO THE GROUND.

⚠ Lowering off

The method of topping out or lowering off discussed on the left works well when you are tying on to chains or to large bolt hangers with rounded eyes. Some hangers, however — especially those made of aluminium — have sharp edges. Lowering off by having your rope run through these could, in fact, cause the rope to be cut through, resulting in a fatal injury. The only alternatives here are:

■ To leave a carabiner or carabiners at the top
■ To carry cheap shackles you can leave at the top
■ To thread a piece of accessory cord — no thinner than 6mm (3/8 in) — through both hangers, pull half your rope up, feed it through the cord, and rappel very carefully using both ropes. *Do not attempt to lower off through accessory cord — the rope-on-rope friction will cut through it like butter!*

above left A FORCED RAPPEL OFF A SINGLE BOLT ON ACCESSORY CORD (AS DEMONSTRATED HERE), IS AN ABSOLUTE LAST RESORT.

above right SHARP-EDGED HANGERS CAN CAUSE ROPE TO FRAY.

Cleaning the route

If you are cleaning the route (that is, removing the quickdraws you clipped on the way up), then clip a quickdraw onto your harness and onto the rope before lowering off. This enables you to follow the rope even if it goes sideways, or under an overhang. Watch out when unclipping the last quickdraw (the one closest to the ground) — if the route overhangs, you could end up accidentally 'meeting' some nearby trees, rocks or even other people.

REMOVING QUICKDRAWS CAN BE QUITE STRENUOUS. 'BOUNCING IN' BY PULLING ON THE QUICKDRAW ALLOWS ONE TO MORE EASILY UNCLIP IT.

Special hints for sport belayers

In sport climbing, if the pitch starts on level ground and the belayer can't fall off, down or into anything, then it is not usual for him or her to tie on to ground anchors. The belayer can then make the leader's life easier, by moving to the left or right as the leader starts climbing, keeping the rope clear. The belayer can also move forward and back to give slack or tight rope, as required. Great care must be taken not to carry this movement too far back, however, as in the event of a fall, the belayer can be dragged forward into the cliff — a frequent occurrence, and not without danger to the leader, as the belayer's natural reaction is to let go of the rope to protect his or her face.

Bolts — the good, the bad and the ugly

Always assume the worst about bolts along a route you don't know — check the bolt, see how new or old it looks, look at the diameter of the shaft (10mm or 0.4in is the accepted standard), and check that the hangers are secure, not loose. Bolts that have been part of a route for a number of years are highly suspect, so be doubly careful. The best motto may be: 'If in doubt, opt out!' Climbers use mainly three types of bolt.

THE USE OF BOLTS FORMS AN ESSENTIAL PART OF SPORT CLIMBING. IN CLIMBING TERMS A BOLT REFERS TO A PIECE OF METAL PLACED INTO A HOLE DRILLED IN A ROCK FACE OR WALL, TO PROVIDE SAFE AND CONVENIENT PROTECTION FOR THE CLIMBER. IF A BOLT IS WELL PLACED, LONG, STRONG AND MADE OF STAINLESS STEEL, IT WILL LAST A LONG TIME, AND BE PRETTY SAFE IN TERMS OF REPEATED FALLS. YOU MAY NOT ALWAYS BE ABLE TO TELL A GOOD BOLT FROM A BAD ONE IMMEDIATELY, SO TAKE CAREFUL HEED OF THE WARNINGS IN THIS SECTION.

⚠ Bolts are not perfect

Bolts are *not* infallible — under the influence of temperature changes they expand and contract, and may work loose from the rock or epoxy holding them. Never trust only one bolt, however good it may look, for use during rappels or lowering off. Always use back-ups.

Composite units in hand-drilled holes

Nowadays this kind of bolt is rare, but it may still be in use on some older routes, and can be invaluable if you are doing a big-wall route and simply can't find any other gear! It is worth remembering that the holes were hand-drilled by a tired, possibly frightened climber, who wanted to get the procedure over and done with — drilling by hand is hard work. Many bolts in hand-drilled holes simply do not go in deep enough.

The bolt shafts are usually only 5mm or 6mm (0.25in) in diameter and only 2 — 3cm (0.8 — 1.2in) long.

These bolts are seldom, if ever, made of stainless steel. In many environments iron rusts surprisingly quickly — so take care!

Expansion bolts

For the following two types of bolt, the hole *can* be hand drilled, but it seldom is. It is more usual for climbers to use a battery-powered or petrol-driven portable drill.

Expansion bolts are also called sleeved anchors and are usually 10mm (0.4in) in diameter, 80mm (3.2in) or more in length, and made of stainless steel. (In some very dry areas galvanized mild steel is used.) A hole is drilled, cleaned out, and the bolt is hammered in. When tightened, the sleeve pulls back over a wedge-shaped taper, locking the bolt into place. A hanger is then attached. When properly placed in sound rock, this kind of anchor is both strong and durable, and can usually hold up to 30kN or 3000kgf.

Glue-in anchors

Any suitable piece of metal can be glued into a hole using hi-tech epoxy resins, such as Hilti C60 or C100. Instead of an expansion bolt, you can use a threaded rod or a special staple with an eye at the outside end. Staples are becoming very popular, as they are inexpensive and offer a rounded eye for lowering off. (The rounded rod is also more carabiner-friendly than the sharp-edged hanger.)

Both expansion bolts and glue-in anchors can hold huge loads if correctly placed (see opposite page).

Bolt-placing techniques
Drilling a hole

■ Firstly, check that you are not contravening any bolting regulations — written or unwritten.

■ Check that the rock is sound by tapping it firmly with a hammer.

■ Position the hole (and bolt) *at least* 10cm (4in) away from any rock edge, and the same distance from any other bolt on top belays or lowering stations.

■ Ensure that your drill bit is exactly the right size.

■ Measure the length of the bolt, threaded rod or staple to be secured in the rock, and mark the drill bit to this length with a piece of insulation tape or similar.

■ Drill the hole at right angles to the rock (with glue-in anchors, you could drill it slightly off horizontal at a downward angle) keeping the bit at a consistent angle.

■ Brush the drilled hole out with a toothbrush or rifle-cleaning brush to remove all loose pieces of rock.

■ Insert a short piece of flexible pipe to the back of the hole, and blow down it to clean the hole (keep your face out of the way of the dust and dirt blown out!).

■ *For expansion bolts:* Tap these firmly into the hole with a hammer, until just sufficient thread is showing to take the nuts and hanger. Place the hanger and nut on the bolt and tighten. (Placing the hanger and nut

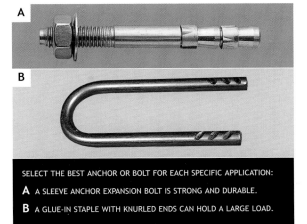

SELECT THE BEST ANCHOR OR BOLT FOR EACH SPECIFIC APPLICATION:

A A SLEEVE ANCHOR EXPANSION BOLT IS STRONG AND DURABLE.

B A GLUE-IN STAPLE WITH KNURLED ENDS CAN HOLD A LARGE LOAD.

on before hammering the bolt in helps prevent any thread damage, and driving the bolt in too far.) Beware of overtightening, particularly on stainless steel bolts, which can shear with over-torqueing.

■ *For threaded rods and staples (glue-in anchors):* Fill one third of the hole with newly mixed epoxy (most now come in auto-mixing glue guns), and insert the rod or staple. With a threaded rod or a straight anchor, twist very slowly in the epoxy to help distribute the glue evenly and avoid bubbles.

■ Glued-in anchors should not be loaded for at least 12 hours.

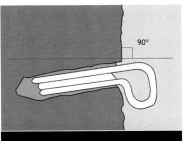

GLUE-IN ANCHORS CAN BE DRILLED OFF-HORIZONTAL AT A DOWNWARD ANGLE.

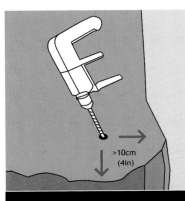

BOLTS SHOULD BE PLACED AT LEAST 10CM FROM THE EDGE ON GOOD, SOLID ROCK.

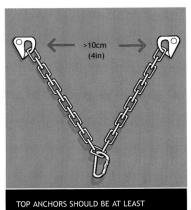

TOP ANCHORS SHOULD BE AT LEAST 10–15CM (4–6IN) APART FOR SAFETY.

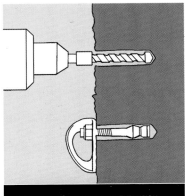

DRILLING AND INSERTING AN EXPANSION ANCHOR IS EASIEST WITH A POWER DRILL.

Leading traditional gear routes

Traditional (trad) leading has the potential of far more risk attached to it than sport leading. This is not to say that it *has* to be more dangerous — it all depends on the climber(s) involved.

The gear

'There is no shortcut to experience' — this motto should be engraved on each and every piece of protection gear sold to a climber. Practice and experience are the only ways to ensure safe leading.

Trad climbing uses much of the same equipment, and many of the techniques, of sport climbing. You have a belayer, a rope, harnesses, quickdraws and belay devices. The difference between trad climbing and sport climbing lies in the 'widgets' you place in the rock. In trad climbing, protection can be broadly divided into natural anchors (like flakes of rock, trees and thread holes), 'passive' or protection devices (like nuts, wedges, pitons and bongs), and 'active' protection devices, called camming devices.

It is usual to hang your collection of devices on a bandolier, which is slung around your neck and one arm, although many climbers prefer to clip the gear directly onto the harness. The latter becomes a bit clumsy, however, if you are carrying a large amount of gear!

TRADITIONAL CLIMBERS CARRY A VARIETY OF EQUIPMENT SLUNG FROM A BANDOLIER, OR CLIPPED TO THEIR HARNESS.

Natural protection

The usual way of making use of a natural protection point is to wrap a sling or piece of accessory cord around it, so look for suitable flakes, knobs or solid trees. Trees, which are often found on ledges, make useful belay anchors.

Tips

■ Simply draping the sling around the natural feature is not always the best answer. Ensure that the sling is as low down the feature as possible.

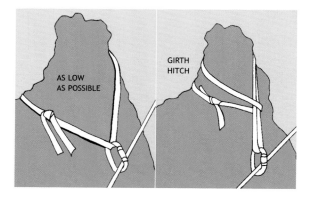

■ Girth hitch the sling if it looks like it might pull off as the rope moves past it.
■ Use other gear to weight the sling if necessary.

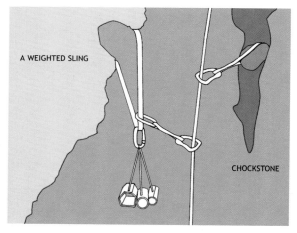

■ Chockstones and 'touch points' (two rock projections touching) can also be valuable — keep an eye open for these when using cracks.

Placed protection

When discussing various forms of placed protection (both active and passive), it is useful to consider the use of pitons, nuts, active camming devices (ACDs) and spring-loaded camming devices (SLCDs).

Pitons

Although seldom used today, a wide array of pitons (metal pins that can be driven into cracks to form an anchor) is available, each style having a specific use: the popular lost arrow is good in horizontal cracks; angles are used in larger cracks; leepers work well stacked in bottoming cracks; and bongs double as large chocks in wide or off-width cracks.

Placing a piton is relatively easy — find the size that will fit comfortably about three-quarters of the way into the crack, then give it a few solid whacks with a hammer. A 'ringing' sound usually indicates that it is solid, although the actual security is determined by the nature of the rock and how far you get the piton in. If the piton can't be driven in all the way, it is wise to tie it off so as to reduce leverage.

Removing pitons

Removing a piton is done by knocking it side-to-side until it is loose. This usually scars the rock.

Old pitons may be sound, but they may not be — often there is no easy way of telling, as the important bits are hidden in the crack! Where possible, back up old pitons. *In situ* pitons are common in the European Alps, and still dot Yosemite fairly liberally.

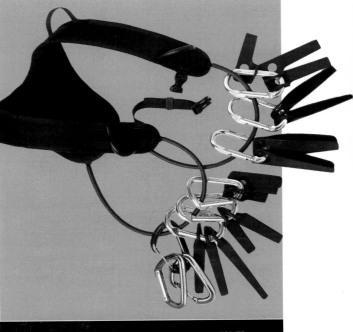

A SELECTION OF PITONS HANGING READY FOR USE. FROM TOP TO BOTTOM: BLADES; SMALLER BLADES; ANGLES; RURPS, OR RPS, (REALIZED ULTIMATE REALITY PITONS); LEEPERS, AND LOST ARROWS.

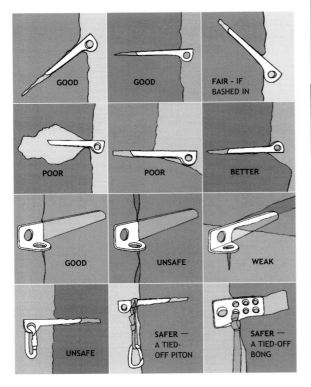

GOOD | GOOD | FAIR - IF BASHED IN
POOR | POOR | BETTER
GOOD | UNSAFE | WEAK
UNSAFE | SAFER — A TIED-OFF PITON | SAFER — A TIED-OFF BONG

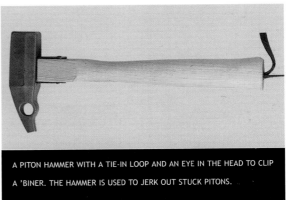

A PITON HAMMER WITH A TIE-IN LOOP AND AN EYE IN THE HEAD TO CLIP A 'BINER. THE HAMMER IS USED TO JERK OUT STUCK PITONS.

Nuts

Stoppers, wedges, hexcentrics (hexes), rocks, RPs and the like are usually collectively referred to as nuts. These are really just sophisticated do-it-yourself chockstones (a natural chockstone is a rock wedged in a crack). Most are incredibly strong, and it is usually the rock that goes, not the nut or its wire or sling.

NUTS VARY FROM TINY (3MM/0.2IN) TO HUGE (5CM/2.4IN), HAVE ODD SHAPES FOR EASY PLACEMENT AND ARE THREADED WITH WIRE OR CORD.

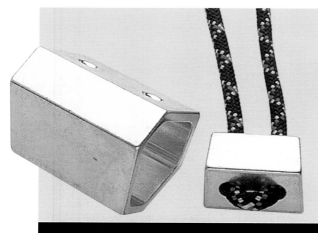

HEXCENTRICS ARE GOOD FOR LARGER CRACKS. THEIR ECCENTRIC SHAPE ALLOWS FOR A NUMBER OF DIFFERING PLACEMENTS.

Placing nuts

Success in placing nuts comes with plenty of practise — sizing just the right nut to the right crack is an art. The best way to learn is to follow a good leader, and check his or her protection as you remove the nuts. This removal is usually done with a nutkey, or 'nutter'.

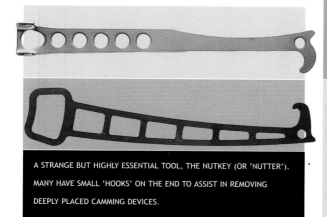

A STRANGE BUT HIGHLY ESSENTIAL TOOL, THE NUTKEY (OR 'NUTTER'). MANY HAVE SMALL 'HOOKS' ON THE END TO ASSIST IN REMOVING DEEPLY PLACED CAMMING DEVICES.

Tips for placing nuts

■ When placing a nut, attach a short sling via a carabiner, and give it a firm tug. This helps to seat the nut properly.
■ Nuts can be placed in opposition to each other (below left) to hold a piece of gear in place or they can be stacked one on top of another (below right).

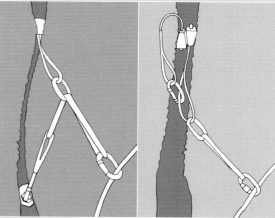

■ Ensure that once placed, the nut cannot drop out of the bottom of a flaring crack.
■ Arrange a selection of nuts of different sizes to a single carabiner — this allows you to choose the correct size, seat it firmly by tugging on the set of nuts, then clip the one you have placed off the carabiner and attach your sling or quickdraw to it.

Active camming devices (ACDs) or spring-loaded camming devices (SLCDs)

These hi-tech pieces of gear are suitable for use in flaring or parallel cracks, although some also work in pockets and a host of other amazing situations. Compared to placing nuts, learning to place ACDs is a complex art. Use too small a unit, and it will rock out; use a size too large, and it may jam in place forever. The ideal placement has the cams at mid-range, and is very tricky to establish.

Tips for placing ACDs

■ Ensure that all the cams are solidly and fully in contact with the rock, not merely touching.

■ In vertical cracks, orientate the ACD so that the axle is pointing in the direction of the expected load.

■ In horizontal cracks, try to wedge the unit in as deeply as possible — with solid-stem ACDs it may be necessary to tie the stem off close to the rock.

■ Remember that the cams may fit better if you rotate the device by 180 degrees. In some newer ACD designs, one set of cams is smaller than the other to hold better in flaring cracks.

Cleaning ACDs

ACDs all need to be cleaned periodically — do this with warm water and a soft brush. Blow dry, and lubricate with a silicone spray — never use oil!

A FLEXIBLE-STEMMED FRIEND ALLOWS BENDING OVER EDGES AND IS SAFER THAN A SOLID STEM, WHICH MAY BREAK UNDER THE STRESS OF A FALL.

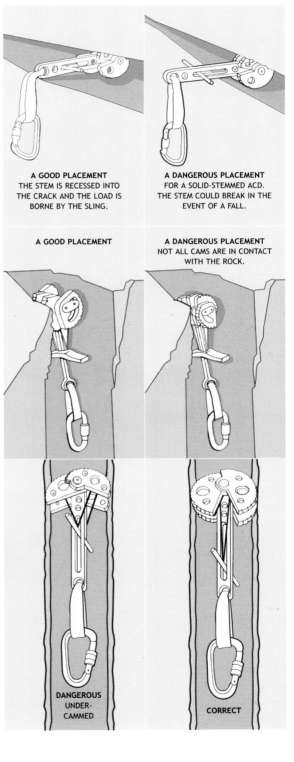

A GOOD PLACEMENT
THE STEM IS RECESSED INTO THE CRACK AND THE LOAD IS BORNE BY THE SLING.

A DANGEROUS PLACEMENT
FOR A SOLID-STEMMED ACD. THE STEM COULD BREAK IN THE EVENT OF A FALL.

A GOOD PLACEMENT

A DANGEROUS PLACEMENT
NOT ALL CAMS ARE IN CONTACT WITH THE ROCK.

DANGEROUS UNDER-CAMMED

CORRECT

■ ARRANGE YOUR RACK CAREfully — normally you place three or four similarly-sized nuts on a carabiner, so that you can slot each one into a crack in turn, and choose the best fit. Arrange small pieces at the front, and

■ Avoid rope drag at all costs by lengthening the slings and/or using a double rope technique.
■ If you run out of gear, 'backclean' by reaching or climbing down to previous pieces of gear, removing and re-using

■ Be thrifty when expending your strength — imagine you are the hero of a computer game, but one where there is no 'quick recharge' of your 'power', and where a serious mistake might mean more than just losing one

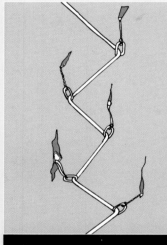

POOR: NO EXTENSION SLINGS HENCE HUGE ROPE DRAG, AND GEAR MAY PULL OUT.

GOOD: SLINGS ARRANGED SO AS TO ENSURE THE ROPE RUNS FREELY.

GOOD: BELAYER TIED ON TO MANAGE BOTH UPWARD AND DOWNWARD FORCES.

larger ones at the rear. Many climbers like to put nuts and quickdraws or short slings on one bandolier, and camming devices separately on another.
■ Avoid clipping both ropes into one carabiner if you are leading on two ropes — differential rope movement during a fall could burn through the ropes.
■ Analyze the forces that — be it through a fall or rope drag — may be brought to bear on the piece of gear you are using, and set it accordingly.

them. Try leaving at least the top two pieces in place in case of a fall, however.
■ Place your first piece of gear soon after taking off. You are not being overcautious — that piece of protection is the only thing between you and the ground, or a large fall, if you are taking off from a ledge! Even if you don't fall on it, the first anchor point acts to keep the rope lined up for the rest of the pitch (see Falling and fall factors page 67).

of your twelve 'game lives'! Rest wherever you can, shake out your hands and arms to get the blood flowing when you can, and don't overgrip — use just enough strength.
■ Concentrate on keeping your technique good, using balance and style, not raw strength.
■ Above all — breathe! When the going gets rough, and panic looms, take a few deep breaths.
■ If all else fails, consider downclimbing a little — every foot you climb down, is two less to fall!

The responsibilities of the leader

The leader is more than just a gung-ho climber — he or she is responsible for the safety and comfortable climbing of the entire group. This entails:

■ Making sure that they all know how to tie on correctly, and have done so.

■ Running through any climbing commands (see page 39) or instructions with the group before starting off.

■ Placing gear so that it protects the second as well as the leader — this is particularly valid in long traverses where a pendulum fall may occur.

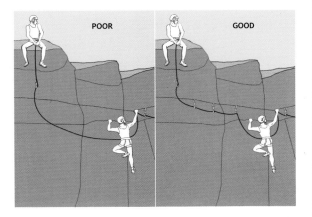

■ Constructing solid belay anchors by never relying on only one anchor; equalizing the load on all anchors by means of slings, a cordelette (see page 38), or rope; ensuring that the anchors can take loads in all anticipated directions; and ensuring that the belayer is properly positioned and won't be pulled up into an overhang, or sideways or downward and off a ledge (see page 42).

■ Making sure that your second knows how to cope with any fall you may have — from trivial to serious.

■ If you are climbing in the back-country or away from other climbers, ensure that someone knows your destination and intended time of return. It is also a good idea to give someone a suggested plan of action to follow if you have not returned by a certain time.

■ Making your party aware of environmental responsibilities, like conventions regarding gaining access, removing litter, making fires, removing plants, disturbing animals, and so on (see pages 90–91).

Falling and fall factors

No one *wants* to fall, but, at some stage, most climbers do. With modern protection, and good dynamic ropes, comfortable harnesses, and effective belay devices, falling is no longer quite as traumatic as it once was. In many ways, falling (especially in sport climbing) is regarded as part of the game.

Falling safely can be quite tricky — and there is certainly no harm in learning and practising how to fall. The instinctive reactions you build up under controlled conditions can help when you fall off by accident under more serious conditions. Using your hands and feet to fend off obstacles, dropping under an overhang without hitting your face, maintaining orientation and not flicking upside down — all these can, and should, be practised.

'Fall factor' is the name given to the ratio between the distance fallen and the amount of rope out to catch you (the distance fallen divided by the length of rope available to absorb the fall). It is the rope stretch that absorbs most of the energy you generate when falling.

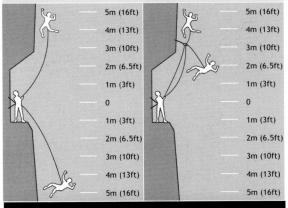

LEADER CLIMBS UP 5M (16FT)	LEADER CLIMBS UP 5M (16FT)
FALLS 5 + 5M (16 + 16FT)	PLACES RUNNER AT 3M (10FT)
DISTANCE FALLEN = 10M (32FT)	FALLS 2 + 2M (6.5 + 6.5FT)
ROPE OUT = 5M (16FT)	DISTANCE FALLEN = 4M (13FT)
FALL FACTOR = 10 ÷ 5 = 2	ROPE OUT = 5M (16FT)
(32 ÷ 16 = 2)	FALL FACTOR = 4 ÷ 5 = 0.8
THIS IS THE MOST SERIOUS FALL	(13 ÷ 16 = 0.8)
FACTOR — EXTREME LOADING ON	A MUCH LESS SERIOUS FALL
BELAYER AND ANCHOR POINTS.	FACTOR.

Rappels, Retreats & Emergencies

many seasoned climbers regard rappelling — descending the rope to the bottom of the route — as potentially extremely dangerous. More than any other element in the sport of rock climbing, rappelling can lead to high drama, serious injury and even death.

The reasons for this are manifold. Many people don't take rappelling techniques as seriously as they should, and don't make the effort to learn and master the essential skills required for safe rappelling. During rappelling, you are completely dependent on your equipment, including your gear placements and your attachment to the rope. If any procedure or technique has been carried out incorrectly or incompletely, the consequences can be disastrous.

Rappelling accidents
Most commonly, rappelling accidents occur when:
■ Poor anchor points are used, and these subsequently give way.
■ An incorrect technique is used to attach to the belay device.
■ A knot failure occurs during the use of double ropes.
■ Not enough rope is allowed for the rappel — that is, the rope proves to be too short.

Rappelling for fun
Despite the dangers inherent in rappelling, it can be undertaken for fun and it does offer a great deal of excitement. Provided all the necessary precautions are taken, there is no reason for things to go wrong. Amongst some thrill-seekers rappelling, also known as abseiling (sliding down the rope in a controlled way) has become a sporting activity in its own right.

Rappelling with a heavy pack
If you are rappelling while carrying a heavy pack, you can easily be flicked upside down if you're not careful. There are some ways to help prevent this:
■ Wear a chest harness to help support the upper body.
■ Suspend your pack below you, attached directly to the rappel carabiner.

IN ALL LIKELIHOOD YOU WILL be using your belay device (see page 40) as a rappel device. Most of these devices produce enough friction to slow you down reasonably. If they don't, then it is advisable to either:

- Insert an extra carabiner brake (see below).
- Wrap the rope around your body.

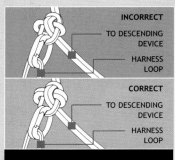

INCORRECT
— TO DESCENDING DEVICE
— HARNESS LOOP

CORRECT
— TO DESCENDING DEVICE
— HARNESS LOOP

PLACING AN EXTRA CARABINER BRAKE.

- The friction hitch allows the use of either one or two ropes, but it does twist the rope, so always use a large, locking carabiner (see page 24).
- However, some devices — like the Grigri and SRC — only allow one rope to be used. Others — like Tubes, Plates and the Figure 8 descendeur — allow for two ropes (see page 41).
- Most climbers rappel with their dominant (stronger) hand as the braking hand, using the other hand to hold themselves upright, or push off from rocks (see bottom right on page 71).

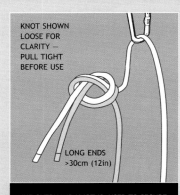

KNOT SHOWN LOOSE FOR CLARITY — PULL TIGHT BEFORE USE

LONG ENDS >30cm (12in)

THE OVERHAND KNOT IS USED TO SECURE THE ENDS OF DOUBLE RAPPEL ROPES.

For the sake of safety, hold your braking hand fairly low down, not close to the rappel device — *and never let go with this hand!*

- Keep your feet widely spaced, and level with your waist if possible.
- When descending over an overhang, lower your body past it, bend your legs, and then gradually slide in under the overhang to avoid hitting your face on the edge.
- *Always* give novices a top safety rope until they are totally familiar with rappelling.
- Use multiple-backups on anchor points — it is cheaper to abandon gear than to pay hospital bills!
- Check and double check the knot(s) used to join ropes. If in doubt, use a simple overhand knot, leaving a tail at least 30cm (12in) long. This is the knot of choice of many guides

and instructors, as it slides easily over edges when pulling down.

- Back up your rappel with a shunt, or a prusik loop.
- Always tie a knot in the free end(s) of the rope(s).
- Rappel smoothly — jerking and bouncing causes the rope to stretch a lot, which can abrade it dangerously on edges, and stresses the anchor points.

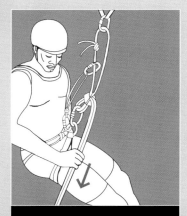

ROPE RETRIEVAL: THE CARABINER AND SLING PREVENT THE ROPES TWISTING AND IDENTIFY WHICH ROPE TO PULL.

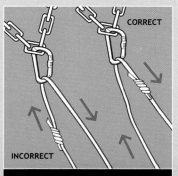

CORRECT

INCORRECT

WHEN RETRIEVING THE ROPE, POSITION THE KNOT ON THE DOWN-PULL SIDE.

Long or multi-pitch rappels

To speed up multi-pitch rappels, send one member down with gear to rig the next rappel. He or she can then fix the next point, safeguard the other members by tying off the rope ends and holding these, and help to pull them in to the rappel stance if the pitch is overhanging.

Tie the rope ends off to the next anchor point before the following members rappel in case of the failure of the top anchor.

Marginal rappel points

If the top points are a bit suspect and the rappel is absolutely unavoidable, then:

■ The last rappeller should use his or her body weight to help support the system (sit or lie on the ledge, or brace your feet on a rock).

■ The second last rappeller should place protection on the way down, which could help hold a fall if the top points fail on the last rappeller.

■ Place very secure anchors at the bottom and tie the ropes to these.

■ The last rappeller should back up with a strong prusik loop (see page 72) or something similar, and a carabiner should be clipped in between the doubled rope, to avoid sliding off the end if the anchors and prusik fail.

■ The last rappeller should rappel very carefully, removing the runners as he or she passes them.

RAPPELLING FROM A HIGH POINT, SUCH AS THIS YOSEMITE BIVOUAC, NEEDS A GREAT DEAL OF SKILL, AS WELL AS IRON NERVES.

USE MULTIPLE RAPPEL POINTS, INCLUDING SOME SET FAR BACK IF NEEDED, WITH THE LOAD PROPERLY DISTRIBUTED.

A GOOD RAPPEL POSITION, WITH THE NOVICE CLIMBER BACKED UP BY A PETZL SHUNT AND A SAFETY ROPE WHILE HE LEARNS THE TRICKS.

Ascending the rope

You may ask why climbers sometimes ascend via the rope. The answer is that it may be necessary as an emergency action, or to speed things up on a long, multi-pitch route, or when bolting a route, or just for fun! All that is needed for an ascent is a rope tied to a solid top anchor, and something that will grip the rope — either some form of mechanical ascender (often called 'jugs') or a gripping knot.

THE SECOND WILL USUALLY JUMAR UP A MAJOR ROUTE. WHEN JUMARING, THE ROPE IS GATHERED IN AND KNOTTED AT INTERVALS, AND BOTH JUMARS ARE CONNECTED TO THE CLIMBER'S HARNESS.

Mechanical ascenders

There are various devices, such as jumars, that help you climb a rope, either by gripping via a set of teeth, or by using a camming action. The shunt is unique in that it can be used to ascend a double rope.

Knots

A variety of knots can be used to ease your ascent. The two most useful are the French prusik and the standard prusik — named after Karl Prusik, the Austrian climber who developed them. These knots are best tied using accessory cord of 5mm to 8mm in diameter, but, if all else fails, use strong shoe laces for your footloop! A longish sling can also be used to tie a French prusik.

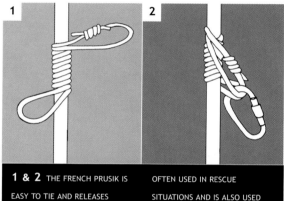

1 & 2 THE FRENCH PRUSIK IS EASY TO TIE AND RELEASES EASILY WHEN UNLOADED. IT IS OFTEN USED IN RESCUE SITUATIONS AND IS ALSO USED FOR RAPPELLING.

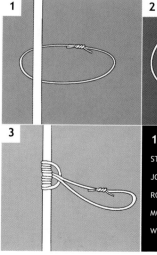

1 - 3 WHEN USING THE STANDARD PRUSIK, KEEP THE JOINING KNOT AWAY FROM THE ROPE TO PREVENT IT SLIPPING. MORE TURNS MAY BE NEEDED WITH A NEW OR THINNER CORD.

Tips for ascending

■ Always remember to let your legs do the work — don't try to pull yourself upward using only your arms!
■ Tying a small weight (a small pack, for instance) to the bottom of the rope allows you to slide the knots or ascendeurs upwards more easily.
■ Where possible, join both ascending devices to your harness — the foot one with an extension loop — to cater for any system failure on the top loop.
■ If you are wearing a heavy pack, either haul this later, or suspend it below you from your body carabiner (see pages 17 and 24).

Down-climbing, traversing off and retreating

If a climb proves too difficult, or bad weather threatens, it might be necessary to down-climb or traverse off the route, particularly if there are no suitable rappel points. Down-climbing can and should, if possible, be done 'on lead'. This means that the first climber places protection on the way down, and this is removed by the second (or last) climber, exactly as in leading upwards. To speed things up, it is often easier to 'lower' the first climber (or for him/her to rappel), placing gear to protect the second climber. Down-climbing is seldom practised, but is a valuable tool in your climbing armoury. Try doing it now and again!

Traversing

To speed things up if the party is larger than two, and the traverse is fairly easy, then you might consider the second and third climber (but not the last) moving across a rope fixed by the leader, by clipping onto it via slings and carabiners (usually two slings for safety). This also allows one to pass protection points and remain clipped to the rope. The last climber comes across on the rope ends and removes the gear as usual.

MOVING A LARGE GROUP ACROSS AN EASYISH TRAVERSE USING A FIXED ROPE. THE CLIMBERS ARE CLIPPED TO THE ROPE BY TWO SLINGS TO ALLOW THEM TO PASS INTERIM PROTECTION POINTS WITHOUT UNCLIPPING ENTIRELY. IN THIS PICTURE, THE STEP-OFF AT THE RIGHT IS ONTO SAFE GROUND.

CLIMBING ALWAYS HOLDS AN element of risk, despite the best preparations. As each emergency situation is unique, it is usually a combination of training, experience and improvisation that saves the day.

'Frozen' second climber

At some stage, you may be faced with a companion who just 'can't make it'. This could be either a psychological or physical inability to complete a climb. Various options exist:
■ Haul on the rope and pull the climber up toward you — this is not as easy as it sounds!
■ Talk (or shout) them through the moves.
■ Use a secure point to tie them off, rappel down and help them.
■ Abandon the climb, and let the whole group rappel off.

Fallen and injured leader

If the leader takes a fall, and is hanging below you, then you may have to tie him or her off, and rappel down to render assistance.

If the leader is way above you, prusik up the leader's rope until you are level with him or her, or prusik to the top anchor point and then abseil down to the leader.

You may then need to rappel off yourself, or to lower the leader to the ground or to a stable, safe ledge before proceeding. It is far easier to lower someone off than

to haul someone up — even if you are one pitch from the top of a 10-pitch climb.

Whatever happens, avoid panic and haste. If you feel you can't deal with the situation try to attract attention, or sit and wait for a search and rescue party, giving what first aid you can.

Escaping from the system

As a belayer or leader you may need to escape from the belay chain to assist someone in trouble.
■ Lock off the belay device as per its instruction manual (1).
■ Attach a prusik loop or locking device to the rope going to the climber — a French prusik is best, as it can later be released easily, even when under load (2).
■ Tie the prusik or locking device to the anchor points using a sling or loop of rope (3). If you use the rope, plan carefully — you may need to use its far end, for instance. Don't be afraid to cut a piece off the rope end if you need it — this is often overlooked.
■ Tie a back-up clove hitch knot (4) or locked off friction hitch (for easy release later on) in the stricken climber's rope, and attach this to the anchors. It should be tied well enough back not to tighten when the belay is released onto the prusik.
■ Slowly release the belay hand, transferring the load to the prusik, and check that it is holding.

■ You (the belayer) may now remove the belay, and release yourself from the system.

Part of the rope is now free for use to get down to the climber via rappel, or to arrange a hoisting or lowering system.

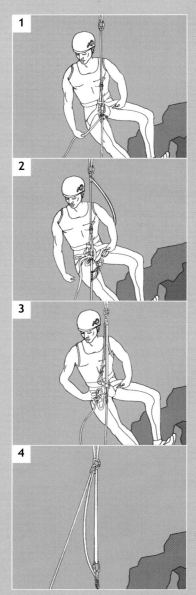

Essential First Aid

The role of first aid is to act to preserve life, prevent further injury or trauma, and to promote recovery. Memorize the so-called ABCs:

■ A is for AIRWAY. Is there any injury to the neck or obstruction to the mouth or nose? Noisy breathing could be a symptom of the obstruction of an airway. Remove any obstructions gently with your finger if this is possible.

■ B is for BREATHING. Is the chest rising and falling, or can you detect the movement of air in the nose and mouth? If there is no breathing, attempt mouth-to-mouth (rescue) breathing, if this can be done without endangering either yourself or the injured person.

■ C is for CIRCULATION. Can you feel a pulse next to the windpipe (carotid artery)? If there is no heartbeat, CPR (cardiopulmonary resuscitation) may be necessary.

■ D is for DECREASED LEVEL OF CONSCIOUSNESS. Is the injured person awake, aware and capable of speech, or is he or she unresponsive?

Further procedures may also be necessary.

■ Check for bleeding. Attempt to stem any bleeding, firstly with direct pressure and, failing this, by using a tourniquet — the latter only as a last resort.

■ Check for possible head, back or neck injuries — do not move the climber until you have ascertained this. You may need to immobilize the injured person.

■ If there are no back or neck injuries, place the climber in the recovery position (see below).

Other things, such as the comfort of the fallen climber, shock, hypothermia, broken limbs, minor bleeding and so on should all take second place to the above major trauma. Don't let bleeding from an obvious, but relatively minor wound, take precedence over more important issues. The splinting of fractures (if done carefully) will help prevent further injury and damage to nerves and blood vessels.

If in doubt, sit it out!

Bad weather, getting lost, injuries, or being overcome by darkness all offer choices — to push on regardless, or to sit it out until conditions improve or rescue arrives. There is no easy answer, as the particular set of circumstances could dictate either course. In general, however, it is often wisest to sit it out. Packs can offer warmth, one can sit on (or wrap oneself in) the rope, and huddling together can offer warmth and security. A small pack containing a bar of energy food, a tiny torch, a small bottle of juice or water, a light raincoat and jersey and a small first-aid kit, could help you avert a tragedy, or avoid a rather uncomfortable night!

IN THE RECOVERY POSITION THE CASUALTY ALWAYS HAS AN ADEQUATE AIRWAY, CANNOT ROLL OVER, AND ANY VOMIT WILL DRAIN AWAY.

Training for Climbing

f or top performers, climbing, like so many other sports, has changed dramatically over the years. With the advent of competitition climbing and the accompanying sponsorship, as well as the sponsorship which now goes with the first ascents of major new climbs, climbers have started taking their sport seriously. With this attitude has come intensive training.

Even if you don't aspire to being the world's top sport or alpine climber, training and fitness make climbing much more enjoyable. The more you put in, the richer the experience will be. Along with the increased fitness and enhanced performance, however, comes the demon of training-related injuries. All too often injuries owing to training could have been prevented, had the climber been working to a planned training regime, tailored to his or her specific needs.

For those who take training for climbing seriously, and would like to develop a proper training program for themselves, there are a number of good books available which offer a professional, scientific approach to climbing training.

Directed training

Beginners often ask what kind of training is best for climbing. Wolfgang Gullich, one of the world's best climbers, said: 'The best training for climbing is climbing'. This is probably true, but most of us can't get to the rocks three or four days a week, and have to make do with substitutes like climbing gyms, nearby boulders and our own training walls or 'cellars'.

The principle of the weakest link

Many factors contribute to making someone a good climber — for instance, finger strength, good footwork, flexibility, endurance, power, mental readiness, and equipment. It was once again Gullich who put this into words. Almost in tears after repeated attempts at a climb in the Verdon Gorge in France, he groaned, 'Climbing is so complex!' He had come to realize that he had put too much time into power training, a domain in which he was already strong, ignoring flexibility and fluidity. All too often climbers ignore their weakest aspects, preferring to work on strengths. This does little to improve their overall performance.

Try to identify the areas in which you need the most work, and focus your training on them. As you improve in one area, so another will require more effort, and

FRANCOIS LEGRAND DISPLAYS HIS LEGENDARY TECHNIQUE IN A WORLD INVITATION CLIMBING COMPETITION, THE ULTIMATE GOAL OF MANY CLIMBERS. LEGRAND ATTRIBUTES HIS SUCCESS TO DISCIPLINED TRAINING.

right BOULDERING IS AN EXCELLENT WAY TO TRAIN FOR BOTH FITNESS AND TECHNIQUE. IT ALLOWS ONE TO MAKE MISTAKES AND TRY TO IMPROVE ON THEM VIRTUALLY STRAIGHT AWAY, AND ALSO REMOVES ALL OF THE COMPLICATIONS OF EQUIPMENT FROM THE EQUATION. BOULDERS CAN RANGE IN SIZE FROM SMALL TO QUITE LARGE AND HIGH.

the picture will keep changing. Proper training requires both self-examination and truthfulness. Locating, admitting to, and monitoring your strong and weak areas is probably the most difficult and constant battle in training and in climbing. With good training, your strengths will continue to support you and allow you to climb, while your weaknesses will gradually become further strengths.

All-round training

There is little doubt that most of your training and strengthening should be directed at the parts of the body that do the most work — but, which parts are these? Before you say 'the arms', think about it carefully — virtually every single major muscle and tendon group, from the toes to the tips of the fingers, and from the buttocks to the neck, is involved in climbing. To train any specific group to the exclusion of the others is to court injury and failure — the whole

JOGGING MAY SEEM LIKE A STRANGE WAY TO TRAIN FOR CLIMBING, BUT IT IMPROVES AEROBIC CAPACITY AND TONES MUSCLES AND TENDONS.

body's muscle groups need to be brought to fitness in unison. Strong pulls need to be balanced by equally strong counter-pulls.

Cross-training has been found to help in most sport disciplines — and climbing is no exception. Jogging, cycling, swimming, aerobics, walking and the like provide both diversionary exercise and general aerobic fitness. Sports like judo, gymnastics and dance promote flexibility and suppleness. Carefully planned weight training can help strengthen selected muscle groups and, contrary to popular belief, does not turn you into a huge, muscle-bound hulk! With the aid of a combination of these activities, you will build and develop a 'balanced climbing machine'.

Rest and relaxation times

Totally 'blasted' muscles need at least 48 hours to recover completely. So, if you train to exhaustion, the following day's training will be worth very little. Pacing your training to fit into your work and leisure schedules is vital, as is understanding recovery time during a single training (and climbing) session, as well as between consecutive sessions.

Understanding what it is you are doing in training

The body is in effect a highly-efficient biological machine. Like any machine, it needs energy, it produces waste, and it requires control and feedback to prevent it from acting up. Its efficiency can be improved up to a point and, like any machine, it can be damaged by overuse or by poor use.

We each have a certain genetically-determined body form or type, and we can do little (if anything) to change the basics. Genetic factors determine things such as the relative density of your skeleton, your height, the amount of body fat you are prone to, the composition of your muscles, the absolute strength of your tendons, and your mental approach to climbing.

The easiest changes to bring about relate to weight (via a careful and sensible diet), and to strengthening muscles and tendons within your genetic limits — which are, in fact, broader than most people imagine.

Improving muscle power and endurance

Muscles consist of bundles of fibres, joined to ligaments or tendons. Each muscle fibre has a nerve which activates it. Muscle fibres are either active or inactive — there is no half-way or half-strength in a muscle fibre — it contracts fully, or not at all. Equally important is the relaxation of the fibre, which involves a complicated set of chemical and physical changes. This in turn depends on both genetics and physiological adaptations within the fibres, which can be improved by appropriate training.

Gains in muscle strength are made in two ways:

■ When there is an increase in the number of fibres in that particular muscle group.

■ Through recruitment, when more muscle fibres are activated to handle a particular pull.

Gains in muscle fibre efficiency (recovery time) are achieved by:

■ Increased capillarity, so that more blood vessels surround the fibre to remove wastes which are responsible for preventing the muscle fibre from recharging.

■ Increased mitochondria ('powerhouses'), enzymes, and energy stores (glycogen) in the fibre which allow faster re-activation.

■ Increased *aerobic* functioning, where muscles burn food more efficiently in the presence of oxygen, and inhibiting waste products (such as lactic acid) are removed in the presence of oxygen. The alternative to this is *anaerobic* functioning, which occurs when the muscle does not have sufficient available oxygen to liberate energy from food — it is less efficient, and produces wastes such as lactic acid which are toxic, and which can only be removed in the presence of oxygen. This lactic acid build-up produces the burning sensation climbers often refer to as a 'pump' — when your muscles just can't work!

Muscle fibre improvement, in terms of both strength and efficiency, takes place in response to the stress provided by training. Regular increased use of a particular muscle group results in adaptation — that is, the muscle fibres start to increase in number, and/or (depending on the type and frequency of the stress applied) each fibre cell increases both its storage of glycogen, and the amount of key enzymes produced. The number of blood vessels surrounding the muscle groups increase, and the amount of blood enzymes undergoes a change.

The training process takes time — weeks, not days — and you need to persevere to achieve results. It is vital to stress the body in exactly the right way to achieve your goals: for power, build on maximum recruitment; for endurance, maximum efficiency in waste removal.

The size of muscles is not necessarily a measure of their efficiency. It is interesting to note that, as a muscle doubles its bulk, its efficiency only goes up by about 50–60%, so large muscles aren't always the strongest. Recruitment of fibres is more important — and this is largely genetically determined. Of interest here, too, is the power : weight ratio (power is relative to the weight that has to be shifted), so lighter climbers can often out-perform big, hulky climbers. This may, of course, be different on long, steep alpine approach marches, or routes needing sheer power.

REGULAR AND REPETITIVE USE OF SPECIFIC MUSCLE GROUPS RESULTS IN ADAPTATION, ENABLING A GREATER DEGREE OF CLIMBING EFFICIENCY.

Of equal importance is the 'use efficiency' of the muscle — this is related to intermuscular co-ordination. Any muscular action by the body is never a result of the contraction of a single muscle, it occurs as a complex interplay between dozens, sometimes hundreds, of muscle groups. Training these groups to act in concert is what constitutes a great deal of training for climbing — building up sequences of moves that use muscles fluidly and efficiently, and with just the right amount of recruitment in each to avoid energy waste or balance and co-ordination problems. This process is called building *engrams* (see page 44).

Engrams

Think of yourself riding a bicycle — you don't have to think about what to do next, right? That is because you have built up cycle-riding engrams, or patterns of movement that allow you to cycle without thinking.

In a similar way, training for climbing will help you build up climbing engrams which will allow a wide range of moves to be done almost automatically, with the mind and body only having to do critical minor adjustments to meet the individual circumstances.

The importance of the mind

It is fair to say that in at least 75% of cases, a climber falls as a result of a mental lapse, not a physical one.

Performance results from a subtle interaction between the unchangeable (like the rock or the weight of the rope) and the changeable (largely the state of the body in response to the promptings of the mind). Every one of us can think of days when things have just flowed — when it was impossible to take a wrong step. This is the ideal state of mind in which to climb — when your confidence simply flows, and you are liberated from any fears and misgivings.

A LIGHT-FRAMED SPORT CLIMBER WOULD PROBABLY FARE BEST ON A SHORT, HARD ROUTE WHICH CALLS FOR AGILITY AND PERSEVERANCE.

A LONG MULTI-PITCH CLIMB ON TRADITIONAL GEAR FAVOURS A HEAVIER-BODIED CLIMBER WITH MORE POWER AND GENERAL ENDURANCE.

At any given time while climbing, your body employs a 'triad' to make things happen: the mind (psychological component), the autonomic nervous sytem (e.g. breathing, digestion, heart rate, perspiration) and the motor nervous system (the muscles you control). These three aspects interact whether you like it or not.

Arousal

In climbing, the term arousal is used to refer to the state of the body's readiness to do something. The level of arousal largely reflects the ratio between *adrenaline* and *noradrenaline,* two hormones secreted by the brain in response to stress. Adrenaline is the 'fight or flight' hormone, which allows the body to override its normal limits of strength. In climbing, this override may be a good thing, but the trade-off is decreased muscle co-ordination, leading to a lack of the fine motor actions needed to climb hard rock. When you are hyped up, the amount of adrenaline in the body increases, pushing up your heart rate and breathing.

Being scared pushes up your adrenaline levels, and increases power, but it also increases perspiration and reduces co-ordination. So, although being aroused may help you over desperate, chunky overhangs, it will count against you on a technical route which needs fine foot placement and tricky hand action. There is an optimal state of arousal for each person for each type of climb.

Controlling arousal

■ Breathe — deep, regular breaths often help calm you, and allow you time to gain control of a situation. An amazing number of climbers almost literally forget to breathe on or before hard routes or competitions.

■ Use positive visualization — close your eyes, and see yourself successfully carrying out the series of moves that are worrying you. *Feel* the moves — the more real you can make the experience in your mind, the easier the route will seem.

■ Take the climb less seriously. So what if you don't do the route? Will it make any difference to your life? Smile — even if it is only inwardly — and chuckle about it to yourself. Get things into perspective.

■ Promote positive expectations for yourself. Don't

think, 'But this is the hardest thing I have ever done'. Rather say, 'I've done many things almost as hard, and I am trained and ready for this one'.

■ Be success-oriented — don't think of how you could fail; think only of how well you could succeed. Repeat as a mantra: 'I *can* do this, I *can* do this!'

■ Relax (de-tension) your body just before you start — spend a few seconds or minutes actively trying to relax any tense muscles — sit calmly, and visualize (and feel!) each muscle relaxing, from your toes to your head.

CLIMBERS MUST LEARN TO ASSESS AND ACHIEVE AN OPTIMAL STATE OF AROUSAL FOR THE CLIMB OR ROUTE THEY ARE ABOUT TO UNDERTAKE, IN ORDER TO MEET THE CHALLENGE OF THE PARTICULAR CLIMB.

Injuries

It is easy for injuries to become the bugbear of training, and of climbing. However, according to a leading sports physiotherapist, 80% of climbing-related injuries she encounters could have been prevented. How?

Avoiding injuries

■ Warm up and stretch — every single time! Even a few moves with an unsupple body could start microtrauma — tiny injuries that normally heal themselves in a short time, but, if continually added to, can lead to a major tear in your tendons at some future stage.

■ Always start at low intensity, until your joints, tendons and muscles are ready for 'the big ones'.

■ Be reasonable in your expectations — it takes from four to ten *years* to train a first-class climber!

■ Stop the instant you feel pain or serious discomfort. Heed your body's warning signs.

■ Beware of cold conditions — these can be damaging to tendons and muscles which are not *thoroughly* warm. Remember that pain responses are dampened by cold, thus injuries can go unnoticed.

■ If there is any inflammation, then stop the activity until it has totally disappeared.

■ Know when to let go — most injuries occur when climbers *know* they can't hold a move, but still foolishly and desperately try.

■ Tape up crucial joints, such as fingers, knees and ankles, *before* they start to get sore.

Treating and recovering from injuries

Evaluate the seriousness of the injury. If you hear or heard a sound (a 'pop' as a tendon tore, or clicking in a joint), feel severe pain, swelling or numbness, stop exercizing totally for five days to a week. Consider consulting a qualified sports doctor or physiotherapist.

Immediate treatment: R.I.C.E.

R — Rest: Immobilize the limb or joint as soon as you can, even if it feels 'better' soon after the injury —this is probably the body's natural pain suppression system kicking in and fooling you.

I — Ice: Treat it by applying ice or immersing in cool water to help reduce swelling.

A FEW KEY STRETCHING EXERCISES. TRY AND STRETCH EVERY POSSIBLE MUSCLE AND LIGAMENT GROUP BEFORE STARTING ANY TRAINING SESSION.

C — Compress: Wrapping the limb or joint in a tight bandage or something similar also reduces swelling, and helps with immobilization.

E — Elevate: Raising the limb above the level of the heart helps excess fluid to drain and reduces swelling.

Long-term treatment: Rehabilitation

The circulatory system is vital in the healing process. Muscles heal faster than ligaments and tendons, as they are served by plenty of blood vessels. For muscles, each healing phase requires some 2—3 days; for tendons and ligaments, from 1—6 weeks is needed.

Phases of rehabilitation

■ *Rest* — this first phase requires that the affected part is not used at all.

■ After rest comes *use* — this promotes blood flow, but it must be done very carefully, and introduced gradually. Careful, non-aggressive movement of the joint or limb should be carried out. *Stop* the minute any sharp or continuous pain occurs.

■ Once the injured part can move fully and normally, then progressive *resistance* (loading) is applied to the injured area. During rest periods, *heat packs* can be used to encourage blood supply. *Warm up and stretch thoroughly in this phase.*

■ *Re-training* is the last phase —the injured part is slowly brought back into climbing mode via a progressive re-training programme, starting at low intensity, with many repetitions, and progressing through to full strength, with few repetitions. Don't hurry this phase! Pain at this stage means 'no!' — go back a phase.

Beginning a training schedule

■ Establish your strengths and weaknesses, and write them down. Ask a friend to help you identify problem areas (and *promise* not to get angry about criticism!).

■ Decide how often, and for how long you can and want to train in the course of a week. Make a timetable.

■ Set long-term goals and targets: these may depend on the time of year you start your training (whether it is in or out of climbing season) and the type of climbing you are primarily training for.

■ Use this chapter (and any other sources) to help you choose a program to address your basic weaknesses.

■ Try to achieve a balance between training for power (short, desperately hard sequences of moves), power-endurance, and endurance (many far easier moves in sequence). Continue to target your weaknesses, but use your strengths, and bear in mind your long-term goals.

■ Set short-term goals to accompany your training program. Say to yourself, for instance, 'In two weeks' time, I must be able to do 40 leg-raises and complete the roof of the boulder cave on its easiest holds'; or 'I must climb the 5.12b problem (see page 92) at the local crag on top-rope'.

■ Allocate activities to your program times. Don't forget warm-up and stretch times, as well as cooldown time and rest periods.

Before each training and climbing session

■ Warm up — do some form of light aerobic exercise for at least 5—10 minutes. Try jogging, skipping, cycling, or fast walking until your heart rate is slightly raised. This should not be a go-for-it, frantic exercise — you merely want to get the circulation going and joints lubricated.

■ Stretch for at least five minutes — general stretching exercises are good, and some specific ones for climbing are shown on the previous page.

Remember that good stretching exercises are mostly static, so don't jerk or bounce the parts being stretched, nor force them to the point of pain. When you encounter resistance, *hold* the position, then try stretching just a little more.

■ Use a few moments after the stretch to mentally run through your goals and program for the particular training session. It is very important to prepare yourself mentally for training and/or climbing.

■ Tape up or brace any problem joints or tendons. Use elasticized strapping or braces on moving joints such as elbows and knees, and use rigid strapping tape for fingers and wrists (see page 50 for how to tape fingers and hands).

■ Finally, if your training session includes climbing — as it probably should do — warm up for 5—10 minutes on easy holds before trying the harder ones.

MONTH 1: Off-peak; 6 months before main season.

STAMINA or AEROBIC ENDURANCE: Do lots of climbing, at low to medium intensity; long sequences of moves which do not stress you or your tendons. Do 50 moves or more; rest for 15 minutes after each set. Climb up and down easyish routes many times. Try very easy routes on lead once you have the confidence to start working on 'head skills'. Jog or cycle for plenty of cardiovascular activity.

MONTH 2: Off-peak; still unfit, but improving.

STRENGTH: Keep on with stamina work, but add half a session of hard moves, many repeats of 6—12-move sequences which at first try you just cannot manage. Start bouldering and continue with it for the next few months. Avoid tiny grips, so as to keep your still-unready tendons in shape. Some directed weight training can be useful, but avoid heavy weights. Try to improve your suppleness.

MONTH 3: Fitness increasing, strength improved, stamina high — a crucial month.

ANAEROBIC ENDURANCE AND POWER: Devote 25% of training to stamina work, 25% to strength and 25% to anaerobic training (routes 15—40 moves long, at high intensity, where muscles don't get sufficient recovery time during the climb). Do interval training (10—20-move sequence, rest 1 minute; repeat 3 times. Rest 15 minutes, begin a new set), increasing gradually. Add 25% power training (short 3—6-move sequences that push you to your max; rest 15 minutes, repeat).

MONTH 4: Reinforce engrams and start getting in tune for the peak season.

GETTING IT TOGETHER: On the wall or rock face, do plenty of routes from easy to just below your max, preferably on top-rope so you are relaxed. To keep leading skills sharp, do easy leads progressing to harder ones. Devote one weekly session to strength and power training (to avoid reinforcing bad engrams which result from 'climbing tired') and anaerobic endurance — this can be a bouldering session, with hard problems first, then laps of easier problems.

MONTHS 5 — 6: Main season. Set realistic goals but don't forget rest periods.

TECHNIQUE, MENTAL AND PHYSICAL: Tackle hard routes. Before climbing, stretch, warm up, and psyche up. Visualize your route plan, make sure you are prepared. Let your firm training base give you confidence. Take a few days off the 'hard stuff' every now and again to rest, and climb something easier or different — if you are on trad, try sport; if bouldering has been your thing, do climbing walls or top-rope. Drop your grades a bit, and just have fun!

MONTH 7: Post-season. Many climbers now take a breather, and call a halt to serious climbing for a while. This enables you to tackle a second season, which may involve something quite different, like ice climbing, deep-water soloing, or climbing in a different region or country.

THE 'HEAD': During this month, turn your mind off serious climbing. Do light climbs, to keep your hand in. A complete break from your normal hard training and climbing routine is often a good idea.

MONTH 8: Pre-second season. If you took it easy last month, you should feel rested, and ready to get back to climbing again.

STRENGTH AND POWER: This goes fastest; so concentrate on this — bouldering is a good idea. Watch the tendons, warm up extra well. Stamina and endurance training should still occupy 50% of your training. Many repetitions of short sequences of moves done when still fresh will reinforce good engrams. Do not overtrain in this phase.

MONTHS 9 — 10: Second season; back to the cliffs. Return to an unfinished project, or visit a new area. Listen to your body — if it is ready for the 'big one', then go for it, otherwise work gradually until both your body and mind agree that you are fit.

TECHNIQUE: A climb seldom succumbs to bad technique — focus on this. By thinking out your problem and a solution strategy, you may just crack it. Be prepared to lower your grades in an effort to climb with better technique.

MONTH 11: Consolidation month; evaluate your strengths and weaknesses.
CORRECTIVE TRAINING: If power was your weakness, start a solid base for next year; practise refining techniques while you still have good strength and stamina. Engrams can only be established if you work on them from a position of strength (repeating moves when fatigued, or using bad technique, builds up poor engrams). If the mind was the problem, begin with easy leads to build up your confidence. Ask friends to point out your strengths — it will make a difference!

MONTH 12: Time for a break — drop your climbing to once a week or so. Let your body truly recover, and you will come back hungry for the rock!

Note: This schedule assumes a 7-day cycle incorporating a 2-day weekend when most of your climbing will be done, and a 12-month cycle with a peak season of about three months. It is for pure rock climbing: thus for competitions or alpine climbing, the emphasis may need to vary a little.

The Way Forward

at this point you may feel that you're ready to try out the sport of climbing — so how do you go about getting started?

- Join a climbing club/school with trained instructors.
- Join some experienced climbers on an outing.
- Try some moves at a rock-gym or climbing wall.
- Find a like-minded friend, and set off on your own.

The first option is undoubtedly the safest, and is highly recommended. It also the most costly, although this cost is relatively small compared to the benefits.

The second is a good one, *if* you can get the climbers to take you on, and if they are safe climbers themselves! Not all 'old' or 'experienced' climbers are good teachers. Gathering experience under the watchful eye of others, however, is certainly a good way to start.

The last option is the most adventurous, but obviously also potentially the most dangerous. This is not to say 'don't do it' — rock climbing is an adventure activity, and true adventure activities have a built-in risk factor. The trick is to reduce the risk as far as possible without diluting the sense of adventure.

Whatever your choice, always keep the risk factor under control. Perhaps the most important way to do this is *to check and double-check* — harnesses, knots, anchor and belay points — everything. And have fun!

right A CLIMBER HIGH ON THE TOTEM POLE, A FORMIDABLE, BUT STUNNING, SEA STACK IN TASMANIA. A LARGE NUMBER OF THESE AMAZING SHEER ROCK FORMATIONS OCCUR OFF THE TASMANIAN COAST.

A THOROUGHLY WELL-SPOTTED BOBBI BENSON BOULDERING IN HEUCO TANKS, TEXAS. THE USA HAS A STAGGERING RANGE OF EXCITING CLIMBING, FROM BOULDERING THROUGH TO BIG WALLS AND ICE.

CLIMBING ABOVE WATER IN GOGARTH, WALES, REPRESENTS ADVENTURE CLIMBING IN ITS FULLEST SENSE — SUPERB EXPOSURE, TRICKY ROCK AND EVEN TRICKIER PROTECTION, IN LINE WITH UK TRADITIONS!

CLIMBING ON THE SUPERB LIMESTONE IN HALONG BAY, VIETNAM. WATER RUNNELS, SCOOPS AND INCREDIBLE STALACTITES – PLUS AN EXOTIC LOCATION – MAKE THIS A DESIRABLE SPORT CLIMBING DESTINATION.

SMITH ROCKS IN OREGON, USA. YET ANOTHER STUNNING AMERICAN DESERT SITE WITH VAST AMOUNTS OF SANDSTONE ROCK FOR BOTH TRAD AND SPORT CLIMBERS.

THE SOARING GRANITE WALLS OF EL CAPITAN IN YOSEMITE, USA, ARE JUSTIFIABLY WORLD-FAMOUS AS THE SITE TO DO BIG WALL ROUTES, EITHER ON AID OR AS A FREE CLIMB.

THE COASTAL AREA OF FINALE LIGURA, LIKE MANY SIMILAR AREAS IN ITALY, HAS A NUMBER OF FINE LIMESTONE CRAGS CATERING FOR EVERY LEVEL OF SPORT CLIMBING.

A CLIMBER ON THE CLASSIC ROUTE, COMES THE DERVISH, IN THE SLATE
QUARRIES OF NORTH WALES. THIS IS A BOLD AND 'NECKY' CLIMB ON
THE NOTORIOUSLY-SLIPPERY SLATE.

VERDON GORGE IN SOUTHERN FRANCE IS RECKONED TO BE THE SPORT
CLIMBER'S PARADISE, WITH HUNDREDS OF LONG, BOLTED ROUTES IN
EVERY CONCEIVABLE GRADE.

THE HARD COMPACT SANDSTONE OF CAPE TOWN'S FAMOUS TABLE
MOUNTAIN, OFFERS SUPERB 'ADVENTUROUS' CLIMBING, DESPITE IT
BEING IN THE HEART OF A CITY.

CHAMONIX, ON THE FRENCH-ITALIAN-SWISS BORDER, WHERE OBJECTIVE
FACTORS SUCH AS GLACIERS AND ICE CLIMBING JOIN THE CHALLENGES
OF PURE ROCK, IS A PERFECT PLAYGROUND FOR ALPINE CLIMBERS.

SOME CLIMBERS MAKE FALSE claims about their climbing prowess, and this can lead to vehement reaction from others. But why the fuss? After all, climbing is 'just a game'. This is true, but like all sports, climbing has its own rules and ethics, and it is these standards of behaviour, usually unwritten, but fairly well understood, that are at stake.

Some very famous climbers have 'broken the rules', or are thought to have done so — debates still rage about the long bolt ladder which the Italian, Cesare Maestri, used to claim the first ascent of the storm-tossed Cerro Torre in Patagonia. Questions are also raised about the ascent of the south face of Lhotse in the Himalayas by the Slovenian, Tomo Cesen. But it is impossible to assert an 'absolute truth' — all issues are debatable and relative to the ethics of the day.

Claiming a clean ascent
The current terminology and set of accepted ethics is given below.
On-sight Flash: The route is free-climbed, from bottom to top, with no pre-knowledge ('beta') of any sort, including photos or information from other climbers. Any gear is placed on lead during the ascent. No rests are allowed.
Flash: The route is free-climbed as above, but you have watched someone else do it, or have beta.

On-sight: The route is climbed in the same way as the on-sight flash, but it is not 'flashed' — so you may repeat a section which is too difficult, or rest on gear along the way.
Redpoint: The route is practised first, either as a whole or in small sections. When you are confident

LYNNE HILL BOLTING A ROUTE IN THAILAND. BOLTS ARE AN ACCEPTED MEANS OF PROTECTION IN THIS AREA.

you can do it, the route is then free-climbed in one go (the accepted norm for hard climbs, both sport and traditional climbs).
Pinkpoint: This is a semi-officially recognized term for a climb where you leave gear (e.g. quickdraws) in place between ascents, and then redpoint on this pre-placed gear. In really hard, overhanging sport routes, no distinction is usually made between redpointing and pinkpointing.

What has been said here refers primarily to sport routes, or short rock routes. In extreme alpinism, expeditions, or big-wall climbing, the parameters shift — often what counts is simply surviving the extreme conditions. The true difficulty of the climb, seen as a whole, will determine how other climbers rate your actions.

The ultimate aim of climbers then is to free-climb a route, with no aid or beta of any sort. Lesser ascents leave the option open for future climbers to do the route in this purist style — allowing progress to be made in climbing.

Other ethics and climbing etiquette
In climbing, it is unethical to 'steal' a climb that someone else has been working on for a long time. If you want to stake your claim and mark a route you're working on as 'in progress', it is usual to attach some string — often red — to the first bolt. Hogging a route that you are clearly unable to climb and will probably never complete is also questionable.

Don't imagine that, because *you* cannot do a climb without a hold being chipped or a bolt being placed, someone won't be able to free-climb it in the future. New equipment and training techniques regularly make fresh manoeuvres possible. Leave something for the next generation to achieve!

The environment

Most climbers claim that one of the reasons they climb is because they love nature and like being outdoors. It is important to note, however, that by our mere presence, we as climbers have an impact on the environment. As our numbers grow, so inevitably does the degree of change we make to the natural world around us.

In many parts of the world, free access to climbing areas is currently under threat. Land owners and managers are concerned by the growing number of climbers, and all it takes is one careless climber dropping litter and not removing it, or defacing the landscape, for all climbers to become branded as irresponsible or selfish.

Some guidelines are:

■ Leave the climbing area in the same condition as that in which you found it, or in better shape, if possible.

■ Keep the rock as natural as possible — do not chip it, or glue pieces of rock to it to create holds, or drill holes and place unnecessary bolts.

■ Enter and leave an area along established trails if these exist.

■ Always find out beforehand what restrictions exist for an area, and respect the rules, whether they relate to nesting birds, plant species, bolt-free zones, or other concerns.

■ Minimize the use of chalk to avoid leaving a mass of white blotches, or try to obtain earth-tinted chalk.

■ Practise minimum-impact camping: use gas stoves rather than fires; bury or preferably carry out human waste; do not wash in small streams; and use only fully biodegradable soap in larger streams or rivers.

■ Carry out *all* litter — including cigarette ends and matches.

■ Don't play music loudly or use bad language when climbing in the vicinity of another group — it offends those who wish to enjoy nature in peace.

You are responsible for caring for the environment, and for ensuring that access to climbing areas remains open.

THE MALTESE CROSS IN THE SOUTH AFRICAN CEDERBERG IS LOCATED IN RUGGED, PRISTINE WILDERNESS. IT IS A CONSTANT CHALLENGE TO KEEP AREAS SUCH AS THIS UNSPOILED.

Using guidebooks

Once you start looking for areas to climb, you will find that various guidebooks are available. Good guidebooks are extremely useful, but poor ones can be quite a liability. Good guidebooks are generally simple and straightforward, and offer only the basic facts, such as the name of the route, its grade, the date of first ascent, the names of the first climbing party, and basic information pertaining to protection, crux moves, length, number of pitches and any special precautions, such as 'avoid the poison ivy at the end of pitch three'!

Also bear in mind that topographical symbols used may vary from one book to another.

Rock climbing grading systems

UIAA	FRANCE	USA	BRITAIN (TECHNICAL)	BRITAIN (SEVERITY)	AUSTRALIA SA / NZ	GERMANY
I	1	5.2		Moderate	9	I
II	2	5.3		Difficult	10	II
III	3	5.4		Very Difficult	11	III
IV	4	5.5	4a	Severe (S)	12	IV
V-					13	V
V		5.6	4b	Very Severe	14	VI
V+	5	5.7	4c		15	VIIa
VI-		5.8	5a	Hard V.S.	16/17	VIIb
VI	6a	5.9		E1	18	
VI+	6a+	5.10a/b	5b		19	VIIc
VII-	6b	5.10c/d		E2	20	VIIIa
VII	6b+	5.11a	5c		21	VIIIb
VII+	6c	5.11b		E3	22	VIIIc
VIII-	6c+	5.11c	6a		23	IXa
VIII	7a/7a+	5.11c		E4	25	IXb
VIII+	7b	5.12a/b	6b		26	IXc
IX-	7b+/7c	5.12c		E5	27	Xa
IX	7c+	5.12d			28	Xb
IX+	8a	5.13a	6c		29	Xc
X-	8a+	5.13b		E6	30	
X	8b	5.13c/d	7a		31	
X+	8b+	5.14a		E7	32	
XI-	8c	5.14b	7b		33	
XI	8c+	5.14c	7c	E8/9	34	
XI+	9a	5.14d	8a	E9	35/36	

NOTE: ALL GRADING SYSTEMS ARE OPEN-ENDED – THE ABOVE TABLE REFLECTS THE HIGHEST CURRENT GRADES AT THE TIME OF GOING TO PRINT. DIRECT COMPARISON BETWEEN TWO ADJACENT CLIMBS CAN BE DIFFICULT, LET ALONE COMPARING GRADES BETWEEN DIFFERENT COUNTRIES OR DIFFERING TYPES OF CLIMBING. THE ABOVE TABLE REFERS TO PURE ROCK-CLIMBING GRADES. IN GENERAL, SPORT CLIMBS ARE GRADED USING THE FRENCH SYSTEM. OTHER GRADES REFER TO TRADITIONALLY PROTECTED CLIMBS, ALTHOUGH THIS RULE IS NOT HARD AND FAST. BEFORE CLIMBING, CHECK WHETHER THE CLIMB IS FULLY BOLT-PROTECTED OR REQUIRES TRADITIONAL GEAR.

Bouldering

Fontainebleau, near Paris, is considered to be the home of modern bouldering. Grading is usually done according to the French Fontainebleau Power Scale — rated from Font 6a to Font 9a; and/or the American Vermin scale, from V1 to V14.

Aid climbing

Aid climbing is rated from A0 ('pulling' on a piece of gear to help you get past a difficult move) to A5 (very dangerous aid climbing, with the potential of a fatal fall).

Alpine grades

Alpine-scale routes are given an overall grade based on a number of systems. The German scale goes from grades I to VI; and the French scale ranges from F — *facile* (easy), PD — *peu difficile* (moderately difficult), AD — *assez difficile* (fairly difficult), D — *difficile* (difficult), TD — *trés difficile* (very difficult) to ED —

extrèmement difficile (extremely difficult), with ABO — *abominable* (abominable) added as a super-hard grade. These grades refer to the overall difficulty of a route, and don't reflect the hardest move.

Mixed routes

Routes that incorporate pure rock climbing, aid climbing, some ice and snow, and other objective difficulties are nowadays rated in a multiple fashion, so a grading of VI, 5.10, A3, WI 4+ is given to *Badlands*, a hard route of 1500m (4500ft) on Torre Egger in Patagonia. Here VI stands for Alpine grade VI; 5.10 for rock free-climbing on the YDS — Yosemite Decimal, or American, Scale — (easy when compared to 5.14 on the warm rock of Smith's Rocks for example, but another story at altitude in a howling zero-degree gale!), the A3 for aid, and the WI 4+ as Water Ice at 4+, an ice-climbing rating. The combination of these grades tells you that this route should be taken very, very seriously!

Topo of Den Vinger

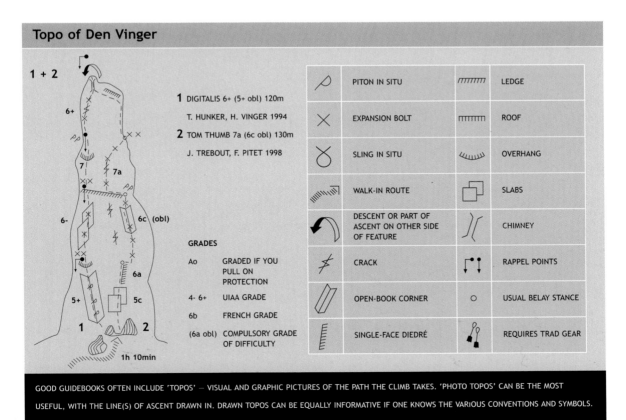

GOOD GUIDEBOOKS OFTEN INCLUDE 'TOPOS' — VISUAL AND GRAPHIC PICTURES OF THE PATH THE CLIMB TAKES. 'PHOTO TOPOS' CAN BE THE MOST USEFUL, WITH THE LINE(S) OF ASCENT DRAWN IN. DRAWN TOPOS CAN BE EQUALLY INFORMATIVE IF ONE KNOWS THE VARIOUS CONVENTIONS AND SYMBOLS.

Making contact

The best way of finding good climbing areas is to meet other climbers and ask them what they recommend. To find these sometimes-elusive folk, you may have to locate and visit climbing clubs, gyms, or climbing areas. If you don't know how to contact other climbers, use some of the suggestions given below.

■ Consult your local telephone directory or telephonic information service to find climbing clubs, climbing gyms or climbing schools in your area.

■ Visit local shops that sell climbing and outdoor equipment, and ask the staff there for information.

■ Try contacting your local branch or headquarters of the Boy Scouts or 'Adventurers' (or a suitable equivalent), or contact some local troops — the leaders often know of local climbers and climbing areas.

■ Buy or order climbing magazines from your bookseller. Most countries publish specialist climbing magazines. If you are interested in international magazines, the most common English-language magazines and their websites are listed here:

   Climbing — www.climbing.com (USA)

   Rock and Ice — www.rockandice.com (USA)

High Mountain Sports and *On the Edge* (UK) — www.cix.co.uk/~highmag; email: highmag@cix.co.uk

Climber (distributed by COMAG, UK)

■ The following additional websites may be useful:

   www.americanalpineclub.org (American Alpine Club)

   www.thebmc.co.uk (British Mountaineering Council)

   www.abmg.co.uk (Association of British Mountaineering Guides)

   www.amga.com (American Mountain Guides Association)

   www.adventuroustraveler.com (variety of guidebooks)

   Many of these websites also contain information on forthcoming climbing competitions and other exciting events which you may want to attend.

   By using a search engine on the Web, you can discover vast amounts of information about climbing, climbers, and climbing sites, including guides to numerous areas.

The Web is a fascinating source of up-to-date news, views and information. The only risk here is that you may get so caught up in reading about climbing that you might not have time for the real thing . . . Once you're ready for the rock, good luck — be safe, and have fun!

Glossary

Abseil *see* rappel.

Accessory cord Thin rope (4—8mm in diameter is usual) used for rappel slings, prusik loops and the like.

ACU (ACD) Active Camming Unit (or Device), a spring-loaded protection device which operates on cams opening and biting into the rock in a crack or crevice under load.

Aid climbing Climbing relying on the use of pegs, nuts, ACUs and other protection equipment for upward progression (also known as artificial climbing).

Alpine climbing (alpinism) Climbing which traditionally implies glacier or snow travel, higher mountains and the ascent of a peak; usually alpine ascents involve self-sufficiency of the climbers and speed in climbing.

Anchor A point of attachment of ropes or slings to rock; can be natural (rock or tree) or placed (bolt, peg or nut).

Ascender A mechanical device used to ascend a rope. Usually used in pairs (*see* jumar).

Balance move A climbing move made without a good hand-hold, where most of the adherence to the rock comes from footwork.

Belay The system used to stop a fall by using a rope — it includes the anchor, the belayer and the belay devices or method. To belay means to hold the rope in such as way as to be able to arrest a fall.

Big walls Long, technically demanding routes usually needing many days for ascent. Not every pitch need be climbed by each climber, mechanical ascenders often being used by the second climber to follow the leader.

Bolt A metal expansion bolt, glued or fastened into a pre-drilled hole in the rock face; used for belays or for running protection.

Bouldering Unroped climbing on any small rock face or surface, including climbing walls.

Camming device *see* ACU.

Carabiner (crab) A metal device which can open on one side (the gate); used to attach protection to slings or ropes, or for general uses in climbing where a device that opens is needed.

CE A European standard safety marking compulsory on all protective equipment (like climbing gear).

Chalk Powder used to dry perspiration from hands.

Chock *see* nut.

Descendeur A device used to increase friction and yet allow the rope to move during a rappel.

Flash To ascend a route on sight with no rests or falls, but with the advantage of pre-knowledge of crucial moves.

Gear General name for climbing equipment, but usually used to refer to protection equipment.

Grade The difficulty rating given to a climb or route by consensus of climbers.

Hexcentric (hex) A passive, six-sided device that can be cammed into parallel-sided cracks as well as used in tapered cracks.

Jam Wedging hands, feet (or other body parts) into a crack to gain purchase.

Jumar The original make of ascender; a toothed, metal device which clamps onto the rope and has since given its name to the technique of ascending ropes by means of similar ascenders.

Karabiner (krab) *see* carabiner.

Kernmantel (rope) Nylon or perlon rope with a 'core and sheath' construction.

Layback Method of ascending a crack or edge where the hands grip and pull while the feet provide opposing counterforce.

Natural gear Protection that is placed by the leader and removed by the second e.g. nuts and ACUs (not pre-drilled bolts or pegs).

Nut Name for a metal wedge or chock designed to offer protection in cracks.

Off-width A crack too small to accommodate the whole body, but too large to allow for a hand or foot jam — usually very tricky to climb.

Pitch A section of rock/snow/ice which is climbed between major belay points — often a pitch stops at a suitable stance or anchor point.

Protection Nylon slings or metal devices (nuts, chocks, hexes, stoppers and ACUs) fixed into the rock; used to stop the climber from falling too far, or to anchor climbers or the rope to belay points.

Rack The set of protection carried by each climber on a climb is called a 'rack'.

Rappel A means of descending a rope safely in a controlled fashion, the speed being controlled by friction of rope around the body or via a rappel device of some kind.

Redpointing A climbing style (usually only in sport climbing) where any amount and form of practice and preparation of the route is allowed providing the climb is finally led without weighting the runners.

Route An established climb or way up a mountain or rock face. Routes are named by the first person to climb them.

Runner The combination of protection, a sling and carabiner used to stop a fall is known as the runner.

Second Climber who ascends a pitch after the lead climber.

Slab A large, often featureless sheet of rock, off-vertically inclined; best climbed with balance techniques.

SLCD A spring-loaded camming device.

Solo climbing To climb alone. A solo climb done without a rope is called free soloing.

Sticht plate A general term for belay plates; the original was developed by Franz Sticht.

Technical Refers to all forms of climbing where the moves are complex and difficult, requiring skill, thought and the application of technique.

Technique ('good') An effective method of overcoming a climbing problem using minimal effort and energy.

Tie on To attach the rope to the climber, usually via the harness.

Topo A semi-pictorial diagram to illustrate the line of a route, and various details along it.

Top-rope To climb a pitch without leading it — the rope is attached to an anchor point above.

Index

Photographic credits

Peter Cole: pp 60, 68 (bottom), 88 (top right & bottom left); **Black Diamond Equipment:** pp 22 (right), 30 (right), 41 (centre & right), 63 (right top & bottom); **Greg Epperson:** cover; **Julian Fisher:** pp 6, 8 (top left), 12 (top), 13, 21 (left), 39, 89 (bottom left), 91; **Bill Hatcher:** pp 5, 8 (bottom), 16 (left & right), 17, 45, 55, 62, 71 (top), 79, 80 (left & right), 85 (month 9), 86 (top & bottom left), 88 (top left), 90; **Garth Hattingh:** pp 12 (bottom), 32 (top), 68 (top), 76 (top & bottom), 84 (months 1,3,4,5), 85 (month 7), 88 (bottom right), 89 (top right); **Hedgehog House/Grant Dixon:** p 87; **Hedgehog House/Hugo Verhagen:** p 18; **Sigma/Philippe Poulet:** p 19; **Struik Image Library/Juan Espi:** pp 18 (bottom), 21 (right), 22 (left), 23 (right), 24, 26, 27, 28, 29, 30 (left), 41 (left), 56 (top right), 61 (top right), 64, 65; **Struik Image Library/Clinton Whaits:** pp 20, 23 (left top, centre & bottom), 25 (bottom), 33, 36, 37, 40, 42, 43, 46, 47, 48, 49, 50, 51, 52, 53, 57, 58, 59, 61 (centre right), 71 (bottom left & right), 73, 75, 85 (month 12); **Maarten Turkstra:** pp 10, 11 (bottom), 14, 56 (left), 85 (months 8,11); **Clinton Whaits:** pp 44, 81, 82; **Ray Wood:** pp 2, 9, 11 (top), 15, 25 (top), 54 (top & bottom), 56 (bottom right), 69, 77, 78, 84 (month 2), 86 (bottom right), 89 (top left & bottom right).